THE PRICE OF AN EYE

THOMAS BLACKBURN

THE PRICE OF AN EYE

'The magic spring which conferred on those who tasted it
the powers of poetry and prophecy,
was guarded by a giant in a deep mountain cave.
Odin longed for its gifts,
but when he asked the guardian if
he might be allowed to drink of the spring,
the God was told,
"The price is your right eye." '

FROM THE EDDAS

WILLIAM MORROW AND COMPANY
NEW YORK

Published throughout the world except the United States by
Longmans Green & Co Ltd

Printed in Great Britain by Page Brothers (Norwich) Ltd.

For James Smyth

CONTENTS

ACKNOWLEDGMENTS

WE are indebted to the following for permission to quote copyright material:
Chatto & Windus Ltd. and Harcourt, Brace & World Inc., New York, for
lines from 'Missing Dates', 'The Last Pain' and 'Part of Madevil's Travels' from
Collected Poems of William Empson; Chatto & Windus Ltd. and New Directions,
New York, for 'Futility' by Wilfred Owen from *Poems* (all rights reserved);
Mr. C. Day Lewis and Jonathan Cape Ltd. for lines from 'Four Feathers to Iron',
'Conflict', 'In the Shelter', 'Elegy Before Death' and 'An Italian Visit' from
Collected Poems; J. M. Dent & Sons Ltd. and New Directions, New York, for
lines from 'Poem on His Birthday', 'I Make This in a Warring Absence', 'Especially
When the October Wind', 'Lament' and 'In the White Giant's Thigh' from *The
Collected Poems of Dylan Thomas*, Copyright 1939, 1942, 1946 by New Directions,
Copyright 1952, 1953 by Dylan Thomas, and lines from *Under Milk Wood*,
Copyright 1954 by New Directions; Andre Deutsch Ltd. for lines from 'Not
Waving But Drowning' from *Not Waving But Drowning* by Stevie Smith, and
for lines from *Moral Stories* by David Wright; the author's agents for lines from
'Saying No' and 'No Offence, Berlin' by D. J. Enright; Faber & Faber Ltd. for
lines from *Eros in Dogma* and *News of the World* by George Barker, *The Nightfishing*
by W. S. Graham, *Lupercal* by Ted Hughes, and *Autumn Sequel* by Louis MacNeice;
Faber & Faber Ltd. and Criterion Books Inc., New York, for lines from George
Barker's *Collected Poems 1930–1955*; Faber & Faber Ltd. and Grove Press Inc.,
New York for lines from Edwin Muir's *Collected Poems 1921–1951*, Copyright ©
1957 by Edwin Muir; Faber & Faber Ltd. and Harcourt, Brace and World Inc.,
New York, for lines from T. S. Eliot's *Four Quartets*, *Waste Land and Other Poems*
and *Collected Poems*; Faber & Faber Ltd. and New Directions, New York, for
lines from *The Death Bell* and *The Lady With a Unicorn* by Vernon Watkins;
Mr. Roy Fuller for lines from *Epitaphs and Occasions* and *Meredithian Sonnets*
(uncollected); the author and The Macmillan Company, New York, for lines
from *Brutus' Orchard* by Roy Fuller; the author's agents for lines from 'Inferno',
'Epode', 'Eve' and 'Ecce Homo' by David Gascoyne; the author and Routledge &
Kegan Paul Ltd. for lines from 'The Mathematics of Love' and 'Palinode' from
The Dual Site by Michael Hamburger; Hamish Hamilton Ltd. for 'Storm' and
lines from 'The World' by Kathleen Raine from *Collected Poems*; Rupert Hart-
Davis Ltd. for lines from 'Ballad of Five Centuries' by Charles Causley, 'Iago
Prytherch', 'Evans' and 'Pisce' by R. S. Thomas; Miss Elizabeth Jennings for
lines from 'Identity' from *Poems* and 'Requiem' (uncollected); Longmans, Green
& Co. Ltd. for lines from 'The Loss of the Magyar' from *The Loss of the Magyar
and Other Poems* by Patricia Beer, 'Shancoduff' and 'Canal Bank Walk' from
Come Dance With Kitty Stobling by Patrick Kavanagh; The Marvell Press for lines
from 'Skin', 'Deceptions', 'Church Going', 'No Road', 'Maiden Name' and
'Next Please' from *The Less Deceived* by Philip Larkin; John Murray (Publishers)
Ltd. and Houghton Mifflin Company, for lines from 'In a Bath Teashop' from
John Betjeman's *Collected Poems*; the author's representatives and New Directions,

ACKNOWLEDGMENTS

New York, for lines from *The Cantos*, Copyright 1934, 1937, 1940, 1948 by Ezra Pound; Roturman S.A. for 'Counting the Beats' and various verses from Robert Graves' *Collected Poems*, © Roturman S.A., published by Cassell & Co. Ltd. and Doubleday & Company Inc., New York; Routledge & Kegan Paul Ltd. for lines from 'A Song About Major Eatherley' by John Wain, 'Titus and Berenice' by J. H. Stubbs, and 'Am Steinplatz' by D. J. Enright; Mrs. Yeats, Macmillan & Co. Ltd. and The Macmillan Company, New York, for 'The Second Coming', 'Mohini Chatterjee', 'Meeting', 'Stare's Nest at My Window' and various verses from *The Collected Poems of W. B. Yeats*, Definitive Edition © The Macmillan Company 1956.

The lines quoted from 'The Third Journey' are from *The Seven Journeys* by W. S. Graham, and the lines from 'Notes for a Biography' by Louis MacNeice appeared in *The London Magazine*, April 1959.

I should like to thank

my wife, Michael Hamburger and James Smyth

for their criticism of the manuscript of this book

and many helpful suggestions.

PREFACE

THIS IS not a book about the technique of writing poetry, the purity or ambiguity of its diction, or the relationship of poetry to the art of music.

Without technique there is no poem; I am well aware of that, after helping to select unpublished verse for a recent P.E.N. Anthology. The feeling behind the MSS. we rejected was often real enough; sometimes the writer even underlined it by a note saying, 'I wrote this after my child died,' or 'This one came after my wife went off with the milkman.' If poetry were just a question of scrambling down honest feeling and sincere thought, then we could have produced a collection as large as a telephone directory.

What these writers lacked, of course, was technique, the art of bringing both thought and feeling accurately into the language of a poem, so that the experience which comprehends them both comes alive on the page and is available to other people.

It is not just a question of poems; without some technical skill it is almost impossible to make anything. Experience can no more be transmuted into a poem without an extremely skilful use of words than electricity can be changed into light without an accurate and deft arrangement of glass and wire filament. But technique is only a means. One doesn't usually sit down for a very long time and admire the beauty of an electric bulb as an end in itself. The point is the job that the thing does. The polished machinery of a car may look pleasant enough when opened up for the public view and being turned smoothly in a showroom window. But the aim of the technical skill which has gone into the cylinders and crankshafts is not just a pretty mobile, but a vehicle which has the ability to take us from place to place with speed and efficiency.

This may seem obvious enough as regards machines; but I believe it is easy to forget nowadays that the poem also has a job to do, that unless it is doing this job it is as useless as a dead bulb.

9

Contemporary criticism tends to concentrate on technique. We are told about the startling effects which are produced by a nice conjunction of noun and adjective, the way our senses are stirred by vowels melodiously hooting from thickets of consonants, or our minds by the ambiguities implicit in the word 'BUT'.

Such a concentration leads to the idea of the poem as a 'Thing in itself'. As effectively as a showroom window separates a car from its business with the road, it isolates the poem from its main purpose, which is to make significant statements about what, broadly speaking, we choose to call life. Luckily it is very difficult to withdraw words from their function of making meaningful observations. The attempt, for example, to reduce poetry to its melodic sounds wilts hopelessly before the admirable paraphrase of *Kubla Khan* which begins:

> In Bakerloo did Aly Khan
> A stately Hippodrome decree
> Where Alf, the bread-delivery man. . .

But the fact remains that by considering the poem as an end in itself, a mere question of vowels and consonants, word music and ambiguity, some academic critics have teamed up with popular bad taste. Both of them think of the poem as a pretty but quite useless object for the chimneypiece, the only difference lying in the colour and texture of the ornament, whether it is appropriate to the senior common-room or the purlieus of Clapham.

The point must be emphasised; I do believe there is a tendency to ignore the purpose for which poems are made. Of course there will always be enough tricksy bits of verse turned out to satisfy those who hanker for something charming in itself, and *so witty*. Poets, however, as opposed to confectioners, are not making palatable decorations. Theirs is a more important activity; with pain and difficulty they are attempting to understand, clarify and make articulate the dark processes of human life. Such knowledge is hard to face; at times we all shrink from it; but the fact remains it is the job of many poems.

In this book I am going to concentrate on what poems say; it seems to me there has been rather too much picking about inside them to see how they function and are put together. The point is the work they do. The force of that work can be softened or wholly shrugged off if both our eyes are glued to a poem's machinery.

I

The Poetry

WE KNOW two worlds. One is outside us; it is made of wood and stone, earth, air, water and fire, all the stuff of a material existence. The other is both within us and around us. It is concerned with love and hatred, death and life, doubt and faith, intuition and reason, the subjective experience of a human being.

As our knowledge grows this division begins to dissolve; already we understand how much the body is influenced by thought and feeling, and thought and feeling by the body. Perhaps in time even wood and stone will be understood as but another aspect of the same mysterious energy which sustains the process of man's heart and mind, and the two worlds will be known as one. But at the moment the division exists, and it is reflected in our use of language.

When, for instance, we wish to write about an amoeba or a pebble as material entities, we use flat words which refer to the chemistry, shape, surface and function of the object, prose, that is to say, in its prosaic meaning. But if it is a question of writing about thought and feeling and the movement of the human spirit, then no direct statement is possible. The kingdoms of heaven and hell may be within us, but all religions know this cannot be expressed directly, only through counterparts and resemblances drawn from environment; that is to say through metaphor. Now metaphor is a quality of poetry, and poetry is one of the chief languages of the world of our inward experience.

Perhaps during the past decades, more than at any other time, man's attention has been directed outwards to the first world. His eyes have turned to the things which surround him, and this painstaking exploration has brought about a revolution in the knowledge of environment. This is the achievement of Science, and its discoveries, expressed in mathematical formulae or flat prose, have given those techniques which enable us to use and, to some extent, control the forces of nature. The dividends paid by this domain of external things have been so tangible and immediate that until recently there has been a tendency to cold-shoulder the second world of our inner being. Consequently our knowledge of it is rudimentary, and although we may control famine and pestilence, we may well be destroyed by what we still know so little of, the savage, unpredictable fauna of our own heart and mind.

You may object that if poets and novelists are among the great geographers of this inward world, then in the past decades it has had pioneers comparable to the masters of Science. Blake and Wordsworth, for example, at a time when human attention had already swung from itself towards outer things, penetrated into extraordinary depths of man's nature and destiny. That is true; it is also true that their discoveries are at least as important as the latest ballistic missile or egg-beater. But does it really seem so to us? I suggest that because the eye of the age has been so resolutely turned outwards, even an egg-beater, because it can be handled and does something which is functionally useful, tends to be taken more seriously than some illumination by Blake or Wordsworth of man himself. They write poetry, and because poetry is not concerned with the main interest of a 'practical' man, 'things', it may be dismissed as a verbal pastime with which to waste a pleasant but idle hour.

Good poetry, as opposed to the school of charm and whimsy, can be as referential as chemical formulae. If we do not understand its statements or take them seriously, it is because we have lost contact with what they refer to, that is to say ourselves, all those energies of thought, feeling and intuition which centre on the mind and heart of a human being. It is this I want to discuss, the way poetry can give a local habitation and a name to our inward experience.

When we were children, provided the light was on in our bedroom, its furniture and curtains would be ordinary and safe. But when someone switched the light off and left us to sleep in the half darkness, then quite commonplace objects would grow out of themselves into the menacing shapes of trolls and witches and vampires. If they grew too frightening, then we called out, and when the room was made light again, all the furniture would return to its familiar shape, so that we believed it when we were told there was nothing in the room to fear, and were rather ashamed of ourselves in the morning. But something did happen in that room: fantasies, passions from the deeper levels of ourselves, from the unconscious—to use a contemporary label for this inward reality—fantasies which were kept at bay, or at least curtailed by the firm contours of daylight, were able to grow out from us in the half light and embody themselves among the shadows.

This projection of inward experience on to the people and things about us is taking place all the time; it is almost as basic a condition of human life as breathing. You find its extreme form in the homicidal lunatic. He bodies out the fears and menaces from within himself on to some complete stranger, whom he then has to attack; quite literally in self defence. All of us are continually and often quite inappropriately sending out our loves and hatreds to colour others, so we seldom meet another person, only an amalgam of ourselves and them.

At an earlier stage of our history these inward energies were sent abroad into trees, stones, mountains and lakes, so that nature became the sacred abode of the gods, and charged with 'mana'. Jung suggests that such a naive projection is still going on today, and that in the mysterious flying-saucer, man sees an image of the elusive 'wholeness' he is striving to attain within himself. This may well be true, but on the whole the disciplines of science have enabled us to separate ourselves from our environment. We may find an image for our own uncircumscribed energies in the sea or the north wind, but we are unlikely to perform sacrifices to Poseidon or Boreas. Sea remains sea for us, and wind remains wind, phenomena of an outside nature, although their mystery and turbulence make us aware of similar energies within ourselves. Today it is the inward significance which matters, as if the gods had shifted their centre of gravity from the external plain to the inner kingdom of ourselves. That is their true habitat. But the fact remains that in order to apprehend these gods, or powers within us, we must still project them on to the creatures of our environment.

Tiger! Tiger! burning bright
In the forests of the night
What immortal hand or eye
Could frame thy fearful symmetry.

Obviously the immense force of Blake's poem does not derive solely from its zoological interest. The tiger has become the counterpart and evocative image for those energies, beyond good and evil, which inhabit the dark forest of the psyche. Its creator is unimaginable to us, and its symmetry is fearful, because with our limited finite intelligence we are unable to comprehend such a synthesis of opposites.

The point is that our essential human condition is spiritual and psychological. It is comparatively unchanging behind changing phenomena. But we are also phenomena, a thing among things, and our five senses are mainly adapted to giving us knowledge of what is outside us. One cannot see one's own face without a mirror, and it is almost as difficult to know the processes of the psyche directly. They must externalise themselves and then we can follow the outward bias of our senses and know our inward being through such counterparts in our surroundings as Blake's Tiger, or Shelley's West Wind, all those images which are the stock-in-trade of poetry.

For poets are concerned with an order of existence which can be thought, felt and known, but is not necessarily tangible or subject to measurement, so they must follow its need for external projection, and use images to embody their discoveries. The poetic image acts as a bridge between this inner world and that of our external environment, and through it some unrealised truth about ourselves is able to shoulder up from its shadowy hinterland into our waking consciousness. It is this intrusion into the well-lit, orderly circle of our daily awareness of some new statement from the unlit depths of ourselves, which can make the images of poetry and myth disturbing and at times frightening.

The truth which an image expresses must be as closely married to it as flesh and bone, but the fact remains that an image is not an end in itself but refers back to another order of significance. The White Goddess, for instance, goes through nearly all mythologies. Recently she has appeared in the Ayesha and the She of Rider Haggard; the Anima archetype of Jung is an attempt to understand her, and she is a theme of Robert Graves. She is destroyer and preserver, virgin and prostitute, mother and wife. David Gascoyne gives a picture of one aspect of her in his poem called 'Eve'.

> Profound the radiance issuing
> From the all-inhaling mouth among
> The blond and stifling hair which falls
> In heavy rivers from the high crowned head,
> While in the tension of her heat and light
> The upward creeping blood whispers her name.
> Insurgent, wounded and avenging one,
> In whose black sex
> Our ancient culpability like a pearl is set.

Now there may be women on whom such an image can more easily settle than on others, women who because of this capacity become the centre of very complex situations, and feature in the Sunday papers. But the importance of the image does not lie in its correspondence to any particular human being, rather to some vital and recurrent experience within the human psyche. Certain patterns of feeling and thought from within us are best expressed and apprehended through the White Goddess; she is the nearest external equivalent which we can find for them. To argue about her objective validity is as irrelevant as to suggest a chemical explanation for the tongues of fire which fell on the heads of the Apostles at Pentecost. If this double significance of the image is lost, if we forget it is itself, and yet refers to an order of experience other than itself, then the trees and stones and flowers of poetry become merely an inadequate substitute for the country walk we cannot take because of rain or a sprained ankle. Perhaps for many people they are belittled to just this, reduced with myth and dreams—which after all speak to us almost entirely through images—to a sort of exercise in good taste, or curious whimsy of the lunatic fringe of society. When this happens we have lost one of the principal languages by which it is possible to learn something about ourselves and life's direction.

Of course there are other explanations of the significance of poetry and its images. It is often said that our senses get blurred and crusted up, so that we lose contact with the reality of each other, and fail to see the significance of the world around us. Then the poet, who has somehow managed to keep his sensibility open, restores to us through his work a more penetrating and accurate vision. Matthew Arnold talks about this restoration, which he found in the poetry of Wordsworth.

> He spoke, and loosed our hearts in tears.
> He laid us as we lay at birth
> On the cool flowery lap of earth,
> Smiles broke from us and we had ease;
> The hills were round us and the breeze
> Went o'er the sunlit fields again;
> Our foreheads felt the wind and rain.
> Our youth return'd; for there was shed
> On spirits that had long been dead,
> Spirits dried up and closely furl'd,
> The freshness of the early world.[1]

What is it the poet's vision penetrates; what does it restore? I suggest it pierces the crust of convention and platitude by which we so often reduce a human being, whittle him down till he is no more than his physical presence decaying from moment to moment. The poet's vision restores to us some inkling of what we really are, and suggests the mystery of human nature, shading off as it does into energies, heights and depths which are beyond the scope of our workaday intellect. Creatures outside us, trees and birds, houses and mountains, also have this other dimension of themselves which cannot be measured by mathematical formula or scientific prose. Because poetry enables us to glimpse this other dimension, it restores to Man and Nature their proper majesty and significance.

[1] 'Memorial Verses. April 1850.'

What I am saying about poetry might also apply to some aspects of religion. This is not accidental. A great deal of verse, much satirical, of course, and some narrative, is far removed from religious experience. But when the poet breaks through the speech of his everyday self, when he is surprised by a voice which is more profound than his own and which gathers his experience into a unity he has not yet achieved in his personal life, when—to use a rather shop-soiled word—he is inspired, then the statement made is usually concerned with those powers which lie behind Man, indeed behind all the creatures of life, and are the concern of religion.

It is as if its pressure and energy is so strong that great poetry nearly always transcends individual experience. Even when it is expressing a human situation, such as sexual love or jealousy, it shows the undertones and overtones of the predicament, generalises it, while still keeping the immediacy of real people, into an utterance which has some universal, indeed timeless, significance. However commonplace the starting-point of such verse, rooted in humdrum fact, it will reach over into the more than human mystery which Wordsworth celebrates in his 'Immortality Ode'.

> Not for these I raise
> The song of thanks and praise
> But for those obstinate questionings
> Of sense and outward things,
> Fallings from us, vanishings;
> Blank misgivings of a Creature
> Moving about in worlds not realised,
> High instincts before which our mortal Nature
> Did tremble like a guilty Thing surprised.

The obvious relationship between the poet and the seer is unpopular today and some of the verse makers whom I am going to discuss have lost all trace of it. But the fact remains that most of the great religious utterances, the Upanishads, the Gita, the writings of the Hebrew Prophets, and mystics like St. John of the Cross, use the rhythms and images which are characteristic of poetry. It is unquestionable that many of our most significant poets, Wordsworth, Goethe, Blake, Yeats, are seers in this great tradition, although the recent tendency is to wrench them from their true quality and kind, and see them as something else, men with a brisk eye for a stone and a tree, or social critics. Such an exact observation of nature and society may be part of their work; but if that is all we see in it, we miss its main intention, which is to explore the human being, and show how his destiny expands beyond the small circle of a present moment and conscious awareness, into further modes of existence.

There are today, isolated authors, like Professor Wilson Knight, who have made it almost impossible to ignore religious purpose, even in such a supposedly secular writer as Shakespeare. On the whole, though, we have shied away from this truism. An out-turned interest has been too busy with things to pay much attention to the inward processes of man himself. Scientific medicine and the Welfare State have been the result, as well as hydrogen bombs and sputniks; but a change is taking place. Using the same methods by which we have examined the external world, we are turning inwards again to explore ourselves. This is the significance of Freud and Jung, indeed of all the great psychologists. These pioneers are bringing about a revolution in Man's idea of himself, which is even more fundamental than the change experienced by an earlier age in the knowledge of Man's environment. Between the fourteenth and seventeenth centuries, the geography of the material universe rolled out of its small map into unimagined seas and continents, and the planet shifted its position from the centre of a well-ordered scheme to the periphery of the unknown. Today Man's knowledge of himself is undergoing a similar expansion. The psychologists show, and with something of the scientific method of the age, that our small, well-lit circle of conscious awareness is the minute, exposed surface of vast uncharted areas of existence. And they have begun to explore these areas, so we have a rudimentary knowledge of their first fringes.

> Not chaos, not
> The darkest pit of lowest Erebus,

Nor aught of blinder vacancy, scooped out
By help of dreams—can breed such fear and awe
As fall upon us often when we look
Into our Minds, into the Mind of Man—
My haunt and the main region of my song.[1]

It is true that many philosophers, mystics and poets have always been aware how much more man is than his physical presence and conscious thought, and have written about their discoveries. Their writings have always been with us, and what they say is at least as penetrating as the psychologists, so am I justified in suggesting that Freud and Jung have initiated a revolution in our knowledge of ourselves? I think the point lies in the availability of the discoveries of the psychologist and the fact that his technique resembles the scientific method beloved of our age. The poet has immediate insight into the human being. However, he expresses his insight quite directly; he says 'this is', 'I know', he does not usually support his statements by empirical evidence. No clearer pronouncement than these lines of Yeats could be made about the way children and adults take over and absorb into themselves the opinions which other people hold about them, often quite falsely:

How in the name of heaven can he escape
That defiling and disfigured shape
The mirror of malicious eyes
Casts upon his eyes until at last
He thinks that shape must be his shape?
And what's the good of an escape
If honour find him in the wintry blast?[2]

Psychologists have a great deal to say about this 'projection' of fantasies by one person on to another, who then 'introjects' them into himself. But they support their statements by a great deal of evidence from their case books. Yeats merely utters the

[1] Wordsworth: *The Prelude.*
[2] 'A Dialogue of Self and Soul.'

truth. Such is the usual condition of poetry: It is, and It knows, but the steps which lead to its conclusions are usually left out—at least as direct statement, though they may be implied by the logic of the poem. I believe the conviction of great verse is always justified, but the point is that the out-turned interest of our age likes to have the supporting facts, and when it meets the utterances of poetry, turning majestically without any visible means of support, 'castles in the air' it tends to mutter, and 'in cloud-cuckoo-land'.

These psychologists—and I include with them such researchers into the wider reaches of man as J. B. Rhine with his work on Telepathy—provide evidence. They give scientific professorial support for Hopkins's 'Cliffs of Fall', Wordsworth's 'something far more deeply interfused', Yeats's 'Byzantium', Graves's 'White Goddess', Blake's 'Jerusalem', all those strange energies and directions of the human being which every seer has been telling us about since the first caveman scratched an image on a wall and pointed his dead to face the sunrise.

Psychologists are beginning to rough out a map of the world of inward experience, and so make that world available to the so called scientific or modern mind. By doing this they are supplying poetry with the terms of reference, the clinical data for its statements, which it has always had, but paradoxically stood in need of. Conversely poetry will implement psychology. After the surface mind has accustomed itself to an Unconscious, a Collective Unconscious, an Id, a Super Ego, an Anima Archetype, these abstractions have still to be brought down to the real emotional experience they are distilled from, apprehended by the whole being. This is a constant activity of poetry, restoring ideas to the life they grow from. It gives us back the living union of thought and feeling, and is a bridge between the two worlds in which we are all involved.

2

The Poet

O God! I could be bounded in a nutshell, and count myself a king of infinite
space, were it not that I have bad dreams.

Hamlet.

TO OBTAIN the magic drink that would give him the
powers of seer and poet, the god Odin had to pay a price to
the giant who guarded its underground fountain. The price
was his right eye, and there is an association between blindness
and the gifts of bard, prophet and seer. For the early Celts it may
have been a condition of the bardic calling, and promising
youths seem to have been blinded for the furtherance of their
gift. Tradition says that Tiresias and Homer were blind and, after
his self-inflicted blindness, Oedipus became the seer of Colonus.

This connection between blindness and prophetic power
suggests that we are only made free of imagination by some
experience, usually rather disastrous, which for a time at least
withdraws us from everyday life. Fairy stories are often a kind of
folk psychology and they throw some light on this process.
There is the tale of the unlucky girl who is tormented and finally
pushed down a deep well by her wicked stepmother. Headlong
she goes into the blackness, but that is not the end of her, for she
is able to get on to the best of terms with its inhabitants. An old
crone or an injured fox asks her for a crust of bread or some other
favour, and because the stepdaughter is charitable and helps
these creatures, they reward her. When she returns to the daylight she has only to open her mouth to let fall a disk of gold.

There are many variations of this story. Sometimes a prince
and princess are lost in a forest and the helpful beast guides them
back to their true father's palace, or to the cave where the treasure
lies. The point is that a hostile environment, stepmother, step-
father, witch or ogre, sends the child into the depths of the well,
or the darkness of the forest. Forest and well are images for the
deep inward areas of ourselves which Freud first called the

Unconscious. People retreat into these depths when the outside world becomes too unfriendly, and sometimes they are unable to find their way back to the daylight world, and stay in them for ever. When that happens we talk of incurable mental illness.

But in the fairy stories and the myth of Odin it is certainly not a disadvantage to have made the journey into the interior darkness. Some disaster starts it off, but if the stepdaughter is gifted with the right attitude to the creatures at the bottom of the well she is rewarded with the power of golden speech. Odin may pay the price of his right eye for it, but he is blest with prophetic power, and if the younger son befriends the stranded fish or wounded raven, these creatures help him to find his way out of the forest and to reach the treasure or his true mate. Such stories suggest that although the journey into the underground maze of our-selves—the heights too—may be extremely dangerous, it is the only way to gain personal harmony and bring into some kind of unity the warring opposites of existence. It is also the way one obtains vision. Certainly for the poet this journey is necessary, since it is within the darkness of himself that he confronts the powers of imagination.

It is not enough just to descend into the darkness; that may merely lead to the lifelong wandering in the twilight we call madness. After all, a destructive childhood is rather more likely to turn out a psychotic or an alcoholic than a poet. The point is that the lucky stepdaughter or prince do not lose their way in the corridors and thickets. They make friends with the inhabitants, they wrest some power out of the darkness and bring it back to the light of day. Some people have the ability, innate perhaps, certainly it is as yet inexplicable, of descending into the uncon-scious, and clarifying the energies which confront them there. They are able to yield their own lucidity and understanding to these powers, and by doing so they relate them to reality. It is a mutual process; just as the creatures of the well help because they are helped, so the powers of the unconscious bring understanding because they are understood.

Some experience which has a flavour of catastrophe about it nearly always starts the journey. What is mysterious is the capacity to understand and use creatively the energies of the unconscious, or, to put it in the language of the fairy story, obtain a gift from the creatures of the well, and not be swallowed up by the darkness. This capacity is certainly not a prerogative of poets, nor is the descent; but I am only talking about those poets who have achieved it. Many of us, however, live safely above ground, and, though not blest with any special vision, are in danger of being swallowed up by nothing more exciting than a London bus.

If the descent has been made, if there has been some exploration of the darkness and its savage fauna, then what matters is the ability still to keep a hold on common sense and its reality. That ability is the tenuous thread by which Theseus was able to find his way back to Thebes from the maze of the Minotaur. It is this which differentiates the poet from the lunatic. Both of them are among those who journey in the interior world. Because this is where the river of imagination has its source, the lunatic is also capable of profound utterances, sometimes with the true prophetic aura about them. However, the lunatic has lost his hold on everyday reality, or is losing it, so these statements are fragmentary for him, or a kind of swan-song before he tips over into a psychosis. For a few blinding instants he penetrates deeply into the life of things, before he packs up what is commonly thought of as life.

The poet may not lapse into the interior darkness. He brings it into the light of his mind; through his work he gives its creatures a local habitation and a name, and so relates them to the business of daily life. Conversely, because he knows this other dimension of himself, he is able to comprehend it in the people who move about him, and express in his verse something of the mysterious significance which they all have. The poet has the double vision of the god Odin; with his blinded eye he beholds what goes on in the night of himself; his other eye watches the outer scene. If one of his eyes is not blind then he becomes, at best, just a clever reporter of external phenomena; on the other hand if both of them are blind, he is lost in the shadows. Given this double vision of light and dark, he is able to inter-relate the two worlds and interpret them to each other.

It is not easy to maintain this openness, this perilous stance between the night and day of existence; but it is necessary if a poet is to remain true to his vocation. The danger is to swing too far over into one or other of the worlds and lose the balanced poise between them. For instance, if the poet lapses into the Unconscious and fails to keep in touch with everyday reality then not only will his work tend to become cloudy and fantastic, but he will often degenerate as a personality and become chaotic. Forest and well are not just the abode of benevolent creatures endowed with visionary wisdom, they also contain the werewolf and vampire and are the matrix of the homicidal maniac as well as the poet and seer. The poet—anyone who makes the descent—has to confront both these creative and destructive energies. But he must understand them by the light of his mind, know them within himself as a man. If they absorb his humanity then he becomes like the Minotaur in the Cretan maze, a mere creature of the darkness, with the head of an animal, not a human being. This is what the recently discovered *Gospel According to Thomas* is referring to when it says, 'Blessed is the lion which the man eats and the lion will become a man; and cursed is the man whom the lion eats and the lion will become a man.'

In the case of the poet Rimbaud one sees this danger of being swallowed up by the unconscious. In early life he swung with a desperate compulsion towards it, systematically deranging his senses and conscious intellect by drugs and alcohol in order to be free of conventional discipline and open to every stirring and murmur of the unpredictable. The result was *Les Illuminations* and *Le Bateau Ivre*, a short but splendid flowering of poetry. Rimbaud soon came to realise that the conclusion of his complete openness was madness, and then made an equally compulsive effort to crawl back to the drier land of sanity. There is something tragic in the attempt of this haunted visionary to establish himself as a man of action, a trader in Africa, after his wild journey into the depths of himself.

Dylan Thomas is another poet who was unable to maintain a balanced poise between the imagination and the brute facts of ordinary life, at least outside his fine verse. Personal conflict and the tensions of routine are the drab stuff which the poetic imagination must illuminate. But Thomas seems to have taken refuge from his personal difficulties in a kind of alcoholic euphoria.

Increasingly he dissolved the outer world, or at least drank out of action the conscious mind which perceives it, until finally he was not able to return from the inner darkness:

> Oh let me midlife mourn by the shrined
> And druid herons' vows
> The voyage to ruin I must run
> Dawn ships clouted aground. . . .[1]

The other danger is for the poet progressively to harden himself against the stirrings of the interior world of imagination. If he does this then he loses the blind but visionary eye of Odin. He keeps his seeing eye, the eye of the reporter, and, since craftsmanship remains, can comment neatly enough about the surface of things and current opinion, but he has lost his ability to penetrate through external appearance into those dimensions which it is the poet's vocation to explore. Perhaps few poets went further into those dimensions than Wordsworth, but in later life he seems to have lost contact with them and made conventional religion and opinion a substitute for his imagination. Mr. Wordsworth of Rydal Mount seems to have lived on after William Wordsworth the poet had died, although these words of a contemporary Lakeland farmer suggest that he remained haunted by his Muse:

> He was not a man as folks could crack with, nor not a man as could crack with folks. . . . He was a lonely man, fond of going out with his family and saying nout to noan of them. When a man goes in the family way he keeps together with them and chats a bit with them, but many's the time I've seen him a takin' his family out in a string and never bieing the dreariest bit of notice of 'em, standing by himself and stopping behind a gaping with his jaws working the whole time, but niver no cracking with them, nor no pleasure in them, a desolate minded man.

It is not often that a poet manages to sustain the tension of this double vision throughout a long life. Wordsworth and Coleridge continued to live, but in comparative isolation from their poetry.

[1] 'Poem on his Birthday.'

Sometimes—one thinks of Shelley, Keats, perhaps Shakespeare—the life of poet and man end at the same time. It is possible to think of their deaths as accidental and talk about further directions of their work, but I think it far more probable that their lives were bound up with their poetic vocation and that they died when they had worked it out with some amplitude, or were unable to bear the strain that it involved.

Today it is fashionable to write off this vocation of the poet. Partly, no doubt, this is a reaction against the sentimentalising by Victorian critics of Shelley, Keats and Tennyson. These bards were often swathed in so much prophetic glamour that today we swing in the opposite direction and think of poets as decent, intelligent chaps, no different from the rest of us, except that they are gifted with a rather special skill, word manipulation. Obviously the ability to use words with great facility is an essential condition of writing poetry, but it is only a condition; by itself it no more makes a man a poet than does a wide knowledge of plumbing or of social conditions in Alaska. What skill alone can produce is a competent turner of verse. But although many contemporary collections, highly praised at that, contain nothing but competent verse, this does not mean that the stuff bears any relationship to poetry.

Verse sets down with accuracy, style and intelligence the kind of surface information which a keen eye and mind can skim from man himself and the world around him. Its comments can be extremely witty and subtle, but are something of a pastime, a palatable gloss on information which could equally well be communicated in other ways. It is essentially a matter of what the eye can see of the physical landscape or the surface behaviour of man in society, of good but common sense. As such its range is fairly limited; it involves our everyday intelligence and those feelings which can be encompassed by it. In fact verse depends on the seeing eye of Odin. It is a form of reportage, and since it does not touch through to those deeper levels where there is a strange intimacy between the knower and that which is known, it provides us with information rather than knowledge.

Poets often write verse in their more relaxed moments, but

verse can be churned out by anyone with some gift for language. Poetry, on the other hand, can only be written by poets, and requires the double vision of the god. It is not just a question of being clever with words or having an intelligent interest in contemporary life; in order to write it one must have paid the price of an eye. I mean that the poet must have made the journey into himself and been endowed with the gift of blind sight. That descent does not depend upon an Honours Course in English Literature, but catastrophic experience, and unless someone has endured in this way and acquired the blind eye which can see in darkness, although up to every trick of the trade and verbal felicity, it will profit him nothing as far as poetry goes. For poetry is not concerned with information but with knowledge, and knowledge, as Wordsworth showed in *The Prelude*, even if it is about a stone or a tree or someone casually passed on the road, is always to some extent autobiographical. If Blake's 'Tiger' was verse it would merely tell us about an animal to be found in zoos and jungles, but it is poetry, and consequently it tells us about ourselves.

This does not mean that poetry is a form of egotistical self-indulgence. When Donne wrote 'Any man's death diminishes me because I am involved in mankind, therefore do not send to know for whom the bell tolls, it tolls for thee,' he was not just making a rhetorical gesture. Our intuition that in the roots and foundations of ourselves we are interconnected is being given some scientific backing by the work of psychologists like Jung and Rhine. They give considerable supporting evidence to the suggestion that we are not little isolated circles of 'me-ness' flashing out messages to each other across intervening space, but interrelated, like fingers in the palm of one hand. They are substantiating the perennial statement of poetry that to know oneself is to know everyman.

Such knowledge entails a painful confronting of oneself in all the dimensions, and consequently poetry will never be very popular. But as time goes on mere information, like hair, gets very thin indeed. One grows out of tangible facts and then there is not much left but the interior world which is the concern of the poet.

3

W. B. Yeats and the Contemporary Dream

A PSYCHOLOGIST once said we know little about the conscience except that it is highly soluble in alcohol. Certainly it is true to say we know little about the critical judgment of contemporary poetry except that it is highly soluble in time. There may be absolute standards to judge the quality of petrol or a detergent, but for art we have only the solitary communion of the individual with the work, and the ability of that work to withstand the acid test of time. Time has its own way of dealing with rubbish; but this does not deter critics; far too often we become omnipotent, imagine that we really know, and in this present moment. As a result the history of Literary Criticism records many enormous gaffes.

Critical judgment is mainly cerebral and as such conditioned by its particular moment in time. Much which goes to a work of art is determined in the same way, but there is always an element in it which is free and unpredictable, a leap into the darkness, beyond the past and the present moment. This element is the work's essence of life, that which enables it to survive through time and not snuff out after a few hilarious months, like a fashion in hats or the season's skirt length. At best the critic may be able to recognise this quality in a contemporary work and help others to discover it. But he must be very careful or his comments may misrepresent the work's outreaching intention, and pin it down to the platitudes and conventions of his particular decade. Still there would be no writing, critical or otherwise, if one didn't take a chance and gamble on there being something in one's response which touches over into the future and is not entirely conditioned by current platitudes.

In his book called *Zen in the Art of Archery*, Eugen Herrigel tells of the attempt by a European to master this art, master it in the sense of Zen Buddhism, where it is not just a question of hitting a target, but of spiritual development. To the disciple of Zen the struggle to shoot correctly becomes intimately connected with the process of life, as if the arrow was life energy itself, and the target its direction and true goal.

After months of useless effort Herrigel at last lets fly an arrow correctly, and the Master, who has hitherto been patient but unenthusiastic, bows to him and says, 'That time IT shot.' The remark 'It shot' is very relevant to poetic, indeed all artistic, activity. It suggests that the struggles of the archer were only significant because at last they allowed a shot to take place as it were 'through him'. I mean that the pupil, the archer himself, had, after months of effort, become just as much an instrument of the shot as the bow or the bow-string. In the same way the efforts of the poet are only of value if they lead to those moments—brief and fleeting—where his everyday intelligence, his conscious persona, is displaced by something more than itself, where, in fact, 'It speaks'. In this sense poetic technique is partly the ability to distinguish between the commonplace daily words which rise so glibly to the tongue, and those which well up from a deeper level, or rather which catch the stirrings of those depths; poetry is very much an art of waiting. Audiences used to be rather surprised and amused by the extreme reverence with which Wordsworth as an old man would read the poetry of his ten or so great years of inspiration. That work came from a time when 'It spoke', so it is not surprising he was humble towards it and seemed to think of it as the work of someone rather remote from himself, and much greater.

I have already talked about the deeper levels of the human being where lie the chief sources of inspiration. For many reasons the poet has an unusual openness to them. His great desire is to make articulate and lucid these dark reaches of buried thought and feeling, and so communicate their intentions to other people. You may object here that many people are used by the energies of the unconscious in this way, and sometimes what it expresses through them is pure nonsense, that they are a new Messiah, perhaps, or can change straw into gold; the phantoms of insanity. This is because they have gone blind in both eyes, in other words surrendered their sight of the daylit world, and so lost the power to relate their vision to everyday reality, and make it meaningful. But if a strong sense of outer values, of event and circumstance, is maintained by someone who is a poet, then what comes through him may not be a merely personal obsession, but a meaningful statement, some unfolding of the unconscious which is hovering in the shadows of many people and just ready to shoulder up into the daylight of the contemporary mind. If this is the case, and if the poet has the necessary technique, and serves the stirring of what one might call the Great Dream of his age, with accuracy and fidelity, then later critics will say that Mr. X was part of the main stream of English Literature, and a pioneer of some new movement of thought.

While the great dream of an age is becoming articulate, it is rash to be too dogmatic about the kind of statements it is making. The danger is (one thinks of some early critics of Keats and Wordsworth) to dismiss the New Dream altogether in the interests of a statement that has already been made, or to pick on some fantasy of the side-shows and give it all the big labels. However, W. B. Yeats (1865–1939) has now been dead for two decades, and although his work still arouses strenuous rearguard action and wilful misinterpretation by critics, it does seem to be gathering that kind of authority which suggests it may go on travelling through time. Perhaps of all English poets it was Wordsworth who gave the fullest expression to the unfolding of thought and feeling which we call The Romantic Movement. In the same way I think Yeats has been used by the Great Dream of our age, and has made articulate in his poetry some of those buried thoughts and feelings which are hovering under the surface of the contemporary mind.

The pioneers of a new movement always arouse resistance from those people who are rooted in the old patterns of thought. It is true that since the death of Yeats there has been an unparalleled spate of writing about the man and his work. But, as John Bayley points out in *The Romantic Survival*, the curious thing about this writing is that it tends to concentrate both its praise and attention on certain aspects of his poetry and life and ignore Yeats's impact as a whole. We have studies of the various influences on his style, and studies which try to show how he broke away from the rather florid romanticism of his early work to the sparse language of his maturity. His relationship with Theosophy is dealt with, and his connection with Ireland and the Abbey Theatre. But I think it was Cézanne who said that the artist was the dog of his work, and when master whistled must come, even on Sundays. After all, every great artist has some particular and obsessive vision of which he is the obedient servant. He is concerned with patiently translating this vision into the language of his art, but it remains a whole which is greater than its parts.

A recent book *W. B. Yeats and the Tradition* by F. A. C. Wilson has at last done justice to the central vision of this poet.[1] Hitherto the fashion has been to brush it aside as if it was a trifle embarrassing, the foible—almost the occupational disease, like womanising or alcohol—of a great word master who was unfortunately moonstruck and saw fairies. W. H. Auden says that although Yeats's rhythms and the conversational power of his poetry have had tremendous influence, his vision has had none. He dislikes what he calls Yeats's 'interest in "magic"', which seems to him to be nonsense. 'A. E. Housman's pessimistic stoicism seems to me to be nonsense too,' writes Auden, 'but at least it is the kind of nonsense which can be believed in by a gentleman.'[2]

There is a rather similar attitude to Yeats in R. P. Blackmur's book *Language as Gesture*. Apparently the poet is concerned with the supernatural, and 'The supernatural,' Blackmur writes, 'is simply not part of our mental furniture and when we meet it in our reading we say: here is rubbish to be swept away.'

There is a great gap between Auden the critic and Auden the poet, but these statements do show the resistance of a certain type of mind to Yeats's total vision. Apparently he is concerned with magic, the supernatural, a sort of lunatic fringe of experience not worth serious consideration by intelligent people. But even intelligent people, if they are sensitive to words, cannot help seeing that Yeats is a great master of language, and this leads to some interesting critical gymnastics. Blackmur, for example, attempts to reconcile his conviction that Yeats is the greatest

[1] As also has 'The Iconography of W. B. Yeats', by the same author.
[2] W. H. Auden writing in the *Kenyon Review*.

c

poet of the seventeenth century with a thoroughly justified suspicion that he believed in ghosts, by suggesting that these beliefs are no more than a convenient mechanism, unimportant in themselves, but useful since they triggered off the poetry. This cannot be done. Words are not triggers, or gestures, or even musical sounds; they make statements, which bear either a true or false reference to processes and phenomena within man himself or his environment. If the bulk of Yeats's poems are not concerned with experience which is both real and important, then when their novelty has worn off they must turn into curiosities for the literary lumber room.

I believe the total vision of Yeats's work is of immense importance and that critics who dismiss it as ungentlemanly, or as magical clap-trap, do so because it is incompatible with their fixed conventions of thought and prejudice. Blackmur's 'mental furniture' sounds impressive at a first reading but I suspect it is just this which must be discarded if new poetry, with its outgoing intention, is to have living-room.

In the first chapter I said that for many decades human interest has been mainly scientific, and, as such, concerned with exploring the world of external phenomena. It has cold-shouldered the inner world of man himself, and those more than human processes which centre on the mind and heart of a human being. I suggested that at long last we are returning to know ourselves, and that the psychologists are using for this exploration the disciplines of science. Yeats seems to me a great contemporary poet of this inward world, and if, as I suspect, the further discovery of man by himself is the special concern of our age, then he has a key position in modern poetry. Perhaps the crucial discovery of the psychologists is how much more there is to a human being than his conscious awareness and physical presence. Certainly Yeats was always concerned with those manifestations of life where we are overshadowed by powers which are vastly more than our everyday self, where the curtains of platitude and convention are lifted for a moment and there is a glimpse of the great strangeness of our destiny.

Now although for many decades the main interest of the European mind has been external phenomena, there is a tradition of thought of immense antiquity which is concerned with man himself, both before and after death. It starts in Egypt and India and comes, through Plato and his followers, to Plotinus and Porphyry. It is continued by Jesus Christ and many Christian writers whether Gnostic or Catholic. Jung has shown how it was taken up into the complicated symbolism of the medieval alchemists, and it is followed in Jung's own school of psychology. It is a tradition of self-knowledge, and how this knowledge can purge a man of phantasies and bring him into a wholeness which is capable of weathering out mortality. F. A. C. Wilson has shown with great clarity how deeply rooted are Yeats's thought and symbolism in this ancient tradition.

This does not mean that his work is archaic, but like Jung he is often re-discovering, re-stating in terms immediate to this age, certain truths which are always getting lost or blurred by the detritus of time. Nor does it mean that Yeats took the ideas of his poetry out of old books. He apprehended these truths by insight into himself and other people. He then found he was able to substantiate these flashes of insight by his reading, because similar discoveries had already been made, not only by such poets as Blake, Wordsworth and Coleridge, but back through time by writers of the Religious Tradition—Plato, for example, Porphyry or the anonymous authors of the Indian Upanishads and the Tibetan *Book of the Dead*.

This discovery that the thoughts and images which came to him in flashes of insight were not solely his personal possession, but a common property shared by many people of all ages, led to one of Yeats's most important conceptions, the Spiritus, or Anima Mundi. Jung has reached a similar conclusion, but he names this impersonal source of ideas and images 'The Collective Unconscious'. The difference is largely in nomenclature, and in a poem called 'The Second Coming' Yeats's conception of the 'Spiritus Mundi' is very fully expressed:

> Turning and turning in the widening gyre
> The falcon cannot hear the falconer;
> Things fall apart; the centre cannot hold;
> Mere anarchy is loosed upon the world,

The blood-dimmed tide is loosed, and everywhere
The ceremony of innocence is drowned;
The best lack all conviction, while the worst
Are full of passionate intensity.

Surely some revelation is at hand;
Surely the Second Coming is at hand.
The Second Coming! Hardly are those words out
When a vast image out of *Spiritus Mundi*
Troubles my sight: somewhere in sands of the desert
A shape with lion body and the head of a man,
A gaze blank and pitiless as the sun,
Is moving its slow thighs, while all about it
Reel shadows of the indignant desert birds.
The darkness drops again; but now I know
That twenty centuries of stony sleep
Were vexed to nightmare by a rocking cradle,
And what rough beast, its hour come round at last,
Slouches towards Bethlehem to be born?

In this poem feeling and thought are completely fused.
You must accept it as a whole or not at all. Yet the poem has
many levels of meaning, all of which are relevant. My interpretation is only one of its possibilities. Yeats seems to be saying that
in this present age, man, and consequently society, has lost all
vital contact with the underlying reality which should sustain
him. You can call this reality God, or the Unconscious; certainly Yeats believed with all visionaries that human beings are
its expression and partial metaphor. But today man has lost
touch with the power which should uphold and direct his
personal life.

Yeats found in Plato his own conviction that every two
thousand years or so there was 'The Second Coming', a great
time of birth and renewal. Of birth because in one moment of
this time, at a particular point in space, there is a new outpouring
of the divine energy which lies behind history. But this 'Great
Year' is also of death, because 'The Second Coming' always
takes place when the old order and its patterns of behaviour have

travelled so far from the previous revelation which was their source that there is no life left in them. The old and the new, these 'Live each other's death and die each other's life'. Yeats illustrated their interaction by his idea of the Gyres or Spirals. Thus, the small point at the very beginning of the Gyre of our age would be the birth of Christ in Bethlehem; that is the coming into time of the timeless mystery. The energies pour through this first small point of manifestation and then slowly unwind themselves through time in increasing spirals. This process is European history; it widens out through the first Church and the ecclesiastical hierarchies, through wars too, because whatever manifested itself at Bethlehem vexes the 'stony sleep' of matter to nightmare! not just serenity and order. Today the divine energy has lost momentum because we live at the very end of the unfolded gyre of an age.

> Turning and turning in the widening gyre
> The falcon cannot hear the falconer.

We live at the last, almost finished, turn of the gyre, consequently there is a hiatus between reason and energy, intellect and intuition. This gives the appearance of anarchy since contemporary man has lost contact with what should support and guide him.

'The best lack all conviction,' because until the 'Second Coming' occurs there is nothing to be convinced about. While the worst—perhaps there was some foreknowledge of the horrors of Fascism here—defend the old moribund order with 'passionate intensity'. I have already talked about the 'Spiritus Mundi'; the image from it, which troubles Yeats's sight, is of a rough slouching beast. What manifests itself at 'The Second Coming' may be creative, but it is also terrifying, since it is destructive of the older order both within ourselves and society.

In his autobiography *World within World*, Stephen Spender mentions a conversation he had with Yeats in the early 1930s. Half playfully the older poet suggested we were just entering the political era. After that would come the age of the psychologists, and then that of the spiritualists when there would be no boundary between the living and the dead. It would be the most terrible, but meanwhile the psychological age will be harder for us to bear than its predecessor, presumably because we will have to know all our motives, and will no longer be able to wish away our negative feelings on to other people and so escape from them. One might say the political age corresponds to the age of science. But although human interest may have turned outwards today, away from man himself towards things, our inner life still continues. If we do not know and accept our emotional conflicts within ourselves, then they will stream from us and invest the external world. This, of course, is what happens in our political age. The destructive feelings which we find intolerable are projected onto other people, and Negroes, Jews, people of different religion or skin become the enemy. But now the birds, so Yeats's casual remark seems to hint, may be coming home to roost. In the psychological age war will take place in its true Armageddon, not in Palestine or Russia, but within man himself. These are vast generalisations, and, as Spender says, it is dangerous to report from a casual conversation, but it does indicate the theme of much of Yeats's poetry. The real struggle, and of course Yeats is with all religious writers in this belief, is within the individual, man himself. In the political age, though, with our out-turned way of looking, we are so blinded by the sweep of events that we fail to realise their origin is within ourselves.

> Everything that man esteems
> Endures a moment or a day.
> Love's pleasure drives his love away,
> The painter's brush consumes his dreams;
> The herald's cry, the soldier's tread
> Exhaust his glory and his might:
> Whatever flames upon the night
> Man's own resinous heart has fed.[1]

While writing about some of the ideas and themes of Yeats's poetry one must always remember his dislike of high sounding abstractions, the didactic rant of bad schoolmasters. 'One can

[1] 'Two Songs from a Play.'

refute Hegel,' he wrote, 'but not the Song of Sixpence', and in 'A Prayer For Old Age':

> God guard me from those thoughts men think
> In the mind alone;
> He that sings a lasting song
> Thinks in a marrow bone.

Event, person and circumstance are real, and the mystery which surrounds them; opinion is only a gloss on the experience of living. He avoids the pitfalls of barren speculation by the intrinsic quality of his language, which fuses thought and feeling and often gives to transcendental statements the immediacy of ordinary speech. He also uses the device of the mask, gains a kind of impersonality, and frees himself from the pulpit by letting some mouthpiece, usually rather a disreputable one, 'Crazy Jane' or 'Old Tom' the lunatic, express his profound convictions.

> 'Whatever stands in field or flood,
> Bird, beast, fish or man,
> Mare or stallion, cock or hen,
> Stands in God's unchanging eye
> In all the vigour of its blood;
> In that faith I live or die.'[1]

This short poem seems to gain in universality and impact by the way Yeats shrugs it off on to 'Old Tom'. We might have been a trifle discouraged if it had come from the poet himself in full bardic regalia. Here is 'Old Tom Again':

> Things out of perfection sail,
> And all their swelling canvas wear,
> Nor shall the self-begotten fail
> Though fantastic men suppose
> Building-yard and stormy shore,
> Winding-sheet and swaddling-clothes.

[1] 'Tom the Lunatic.'

Yeats's personal experience is close to the mystical tradition, to the Phaedrus of Plato, for instance. All living creatures descend from some original state of perfection. Man's soul is self-begotten and indestructible, although, lost in the fantasies of material existence, we may imagine there is only the building-yard, that is to say the kind of out-turned interest which produces cars and television sets, and believe a human being is entirely circumscribed by the swaddling clothes of birth and the winding-sheet of death.

Life and its creatures are real, but it was Yeats's conviction that a human being was far more than physical presence or a particular instant of time. In the poem 'Mohini Chatterjee' he expresses this belief of his through the Hindu conception of reincarnation, the idea that some indestructible essence of man passes from life-cycle to life-cycle until we have at last wrestled into a fulfilled knowledge and unity:

> I asked if I should pray,
> But the Brahmin said,
> 'Pray for nothing, say
> Every night in bed,
> "I have been a king,
> I have been a slave,
> Nor is there anything,
> Fool, rascal, knave,
> That I have not been,
> And yet upon my breast
> A myriad heads have lain." '
>
> That he might set at rest
> A boy's turbulent days
> Mohini Chatterjee
> Spoke these, or words like these.
> I add in commentary,
> 'Old lovers yet may have
> All that time denied—
> Grave is heaped on grave
> That they be satisfied—

> Over the blackened earth
> The old troops parade,
> Birth is heaped on birth
> That such cannonade
> May thunder time away,
> Birth-hour and death-hour meet,
> Or, as great sages say,
> Men dance on deathless feet.'

Human Nature is a process, and a process of which birth and death are only incidents. Some such realisation as this gives an extraordinary exhilaration to many of Yeats's poems. In the ending of the 'Dialogue of Self and Soul' he seems to accept every aspect of his temporal existence as his need and destiny and yet—in this lies the joy of the last verse—to know he is identified with no one aspect of his predicament.

> I am content to live it all again
> And yet again, if it be life to pitch
> Into the frog-spawn of a blind man's ditch,
> A blind man battering blind men;
> Or into that most fecund ditch of all,
> The folly that man does
> Or must suffer, if he woos
> A proud woman not kindred to his soul.

> I am content to follow to its source
> Every event in action or in thought;
> Measure the lot; forgive myself the lot!
> When such as I cast out remorse
> So great a sweetness flows into the breast
> We must laugh and we must sing,
>   We are blest by everything,
> Everything we look upon is blest.

This is visionary poetry of the 'positive way'. All the phenomena of life are aspects of the underlying 'ground' o mystical experience. Yeats makes an affirmation similar to Blake's 'All that lives is holy'. In the work of T. S. Eliot we find a poetry which is often concerned with the negative way of mysticism, where the creatures of sense do not reveal but disfigure the underlying reality, which must be approached through darkness and deprivation.

Not that Yeats is unaware of the illusory and deceiving veil of outward appearance, what Hinduism calls Maya. People are real because the soul is real, and our bodies are its metaphor. But we are disguised both from ourselves and each other by a kind of disfiguring cloak, the conventions of thought, and platitudes of sight, which know only a fraction of existence. The cloak of flesh, too, is hampering the unageing spirit, and this is most poignant in old age. One finds the same vision of age as Yeats had, in the paintings of old people by Rembrandt, where the human spirit seems to peer sadly out of its cage of flesh and bone. If only we could see through the veil of 'Maya' then we would really know ourselves and each other. Here is a poem of his on this theme called 'Meeting':

> Hidden by old age awhile
> In masker's cloak and hood,
> Each hating what the other loved,
> Face to face we stood:
> 'That I have met with such,' said he,
> 'Bodes me little good.'

> 'Let others boast their fill,' said I,
> 'But never dare to boast
> That such as I had such a man
> For lover in the past;
> Say that of living men I hate
> Such a man the most.'

> 'A loony'd boast of such a love,'
> He in his rage declared;
> But such as he for such as me—
> Could we both discard
> This beggarly habiliment—
> Had found a sweeter word.

Plato says in the *Phaedrus* that it is the destiny of the soul to regress from the wholeness and perfection which it has known and become involved in time and material. Only in occasional sparks of insight do we glimpse our original and complete being. Such moments, and the Platonic conception of a wholeness we imagine we have lost, are a constant theme of Yeats's poetry. This poem from *The Winding Stair* is concerned with it:

> If I make the lashes dark
> And the eyes more bright
> And the lips more scarlet,
> Or ask if all be right
> From mirror after mirror,
> No vanity's displayed:
> I'm looking for the face I had
> Before the world was made.[1]

On one level this is a song about a girl and her make-up, but it is the 'Thing that was before the world was made', the transcendental thought, which gives an edge to the poem.

Yeats holds that with Death, and Human Endeavour, Sex is one of the three things a serious person can be deeply interested in, and he has written some magnificent poetry on this relationship between men and women. Like Donne and Blake, his sexual poetry, while keeping close to people and their immediate involvement, widens out into a significance which includes, but is greater than personality. He suffered a long and painful fixation on that figure of Irish Nationalism, Maud Gonne, who may have been the 'Proud woman not kindred to his soul'. He only broke free from his Lilith with middle age and marriage, and this long period in the doldrums of passion meant that when the winds did at last blow free Yeats was an ageing man.

> You think it horrible that, lust and rage
> Should dance attention upon my old age;
> They were not such a plague when I was young;
> What else have I to spur me into song?[2]

[1] 'Before the World was Made.'
[2] 'The Spur.'

It is difficult to think of a poet's life and work as separate, since most aspects of the life, however superficially disastrous, seem to further his work. Certainly Yeats's involvement with Maud Gonne, and what appears to have been his comparatively late sexual maturity, have produced some unique love poetry. Usually such poetry is written in youth and, for all its poignancy, tends to be self-centred, the poet expressing the ecstasy and torment he himself feels, although the stimulus is another person. What is remarkable about Yeats's love poetry is the way he is capable of identifying himself with the experience of the man and the woman. Perhaps only Shakespeare has a similar capacity to encompass both sexes in this way, and I find it difficult not to associate this wholeness of experience with maturity.

Plato suggests that the original state of the soul is neither male nor female but a union of these elements. It is when the soul becomes debased and lost in materialism that these blended elements separate out, and we become a man or a woman. Thus the hunger and nostalgia of sexual love would be an attempt to set right this unnatural fission:

> We sat under an old thorn-tree
> And talked away the night,
> Told all that had been said or done
> Since we saw the light,
> And when we talked of growing up
> Knew that we'd halved a soul
> And fell the one in t'other's arms
> That we might make it whole.[1]

Yeats makes a direct confirmation here of the Platonic conception. But it is not confined to Greece, this idea of a marriage between two people being symbolic of a union within the psyche itself. Fairy stories about the goose-girl and her prince, or the scullion and the princess, tell about something more than what happens in a double bed. Their lucky marriage is not just a

[1] 'Summer and Spring.'

yoking of male and female, but of reason and energy, light and darkness, all the warring opposites within one person. Indian sculptors, as well, used the image of gods and goddesses united in the sexual act to signify psychological wholeness. So did the medieval alchemists with their coupling kings and queens, for it is part of the ancient language by which man explores himself.

Yeats's love poetry is far more than a longing for what one imagines one has not got—the one-sided projections of sexual nostalgia. There is always something immature about that kind of verse; but Yeats is able to enter into the experience of the woman. Because he seems to have reached some kind of wholeness within himself, his love poetry is not only about man longing for woman, and woman for man, but a longing which encompasses both sexes:

> 'Three dear things that women know,'
> *Sang a bone upon the shore;*
> 'A man if I but held him so
> When my body was alive
> Found all the pleasure that life gave':
> *A bone wave-whitened and dried in the wind.*

Such poetry has broken free from temporal obsessions, and embraces life and death in a single vision.

It is extraordinary how Yeats yokes in his verse the sweat and muscle of physical experience with his realisation of man and woman as spirit. As spirit our only real consummation may be outside time and material, but the fact remains that we are involved in them here, and must accept all the opposites of temporal existence:

> 'Fair and foul are near of kin,
> And fair needs foul,' I cried.
> My friends are gone, but that's a truth
> Nor grave nor bed denied,
> Learned in bodily lowliness
> And in the heart's pride.

'A woman can be proud and stiff
When on love intent;
But Love has pitched his mansion in
The place of excrement;
For nothing can be sole or whole
That has not been rent.'[1]

The soul can only regain its pristine unity if it accepts and under-
stands the contradictions and confusions of its fallen state. This
statement of 'Crazy Jane' was also made by Plato and the writers
of the Upanishads. It is also a truth of contemporary psychology.

Death is another of the great themes. Sometimes when out of
patience with materialists who thought man was nothing more
than a piece of animated meat and human destiny only an
arrangement of chromosomes, Yeats would make exaggerated
statements about Spiritualism. But although his attitude to
psychic phenomena is far closer to that of Dr. Rhine and the
mathematician, G. M. Tyrrel, than to that of Conan Doyle and
Hannen Swaffer, it is impossible to escape his belief that there was
no real boundary between the living and the dead. I believe
psychology and other sciences will increasingly demonstrate the
truth of Yeats's beliefs. Certainly a once fashionable materialism
with its emphasis on the human being as animated carcass, and
the absolute full-stop of death, cannot live with his poems.
They are permeated by his belief in the continuance of the dead
and an order of spiritual existence which is parallel to the world of
time. 'Byzantium', for example, that great hymn to the divine
and human imagination, ends with a vision of the unborn
spirits sweeping forwards into time and mortality:

Astraddle on the dolphin's mire and blood,
Spirit after spirit! The smithies break the flood,
The golden smithies of the Emperor!
Marbles of the dancing floor
Break bitter furies of complexity,
Those images that yet
Fresh images beget,
That dolphin-torn, that gong-tormented sea.

[1] 'Crazy Jane talks with the Bishop.'

But this spiritual world of which we only have brief glimpses is no more mysterious than any other phenomenon of life. How little we really know about the origin of a dream or a new thought:

> Where got I that truth?
> Out of a medium's mouth,
> Out of nothing it came,
> Out of the forest loam,
> Out of dark night where lay
> The crowns of Nineveh.[1]

Unfathomed powers overshadow our personal lives. We are involved both in a spiritual existence, where Yeats believed the living man is not isolated from the dead, or his past and future, and a world of clocks where we are measured by hours and the reach of our bodies. In a poem like 'The Stare's Nest at my Window', while keeping their own particular significance, these two worlds are fused:

> The bees build in the crevices
> Of loosening masonry, and there
> The mother birds bring grubs and flies.
> My wall is loosening; honey bees,
> Come build in the empty house of the stare.
>
> We are closed in, and the key is turned
> On our uncertainty; somewhere
> A man is killed, or a house burned,
> Yet no clear fact to be discerned:
> Come build in the empty house of the stare.
>
> A barricade of stone or of wood;
> Some fourteen days of Civil War;
> Last night they trundled down the road
> That dead young soldier in his blood:
> Come build in the empty house of the stare.

[1] 'Fragments II.'

We had fed the heart on fantasies,
The heart's grown brutal from the fare;
More substance in our enmities
Than in our love; O honey-bees,
Come build in the empty house of the stare.

The loosening masonry of the building is set against the uncertainty within the poet's mind, so that the crumbling stonework emphasises the psychological unease, and the unease gives significance to the masonry. The bloodshed and external chaos of the Civil War in Ireland is not different from the conflict within the poet. Like his society he has fed on fantasies and been brutalised by the fare. The call to the honey-bees is for sweetness and a creative order both within himself and the world around him. For Yeats does seem in his later work to have made some resolution between imagination and material fact, falcon and falconer, the dying animal and the golden, imperishable bird of Byzantium.

Human endeavour is the third great theme, but endeavour is meaningless unless it is concerned with something which can endure death:

No longer in Lethean foliage caught
Begin the preparation for your death
And from the fortieth winter by that thought
Test every work of intellect or faith,
And everything that your own hands have wrought,
And call those words extravagance of breath
That are not suited for such men as come
Proud, open-eyed and laughing to the tomb.[1]

For death, when all is said and done, is the direction of life, and just as in the womb the foetus must grow organs which are appropriate for this world, so here we must grow spiritually if we are to be ready for the kingdom of death. Such growth is the chief aim of human endeavour.

[1] 'Vacillation.'

His later poems are full of images for resolved being:

> O, chestnut-tree, great-rooted blossomer,
> Are you the leaf, the blossom or the bole?
> O body swayed to music, O brightening glance,
> How can we know the dancer from the dance?[1]

Whether or not he achieved such a resolution within himself is a matter of conjecture. For my part I believe that Yeats did bring some of the symmetry and energy of his work into his personal life. I also believe that no poet since Wordsworth and Blake has more fully achieved the double vision of the god Odin, explored with such breadth and penetration those energies which centre upon man, whether in solitude or in society.

[1] 'Among School Children.'

4

T. S. Eliot

"I dislike the word 'generation', which has been a talisman for the last ten years: when I wrote a poem called 'The Waste Land' some of the more approving critics said I had expressed the disillusionment of a generation, which is nonsense. I may have expressed for them their own illusion of being disillusioned, but that did not form part of my intention."

T. S. ELIOT: *Thoughts after Lambeth.*

T. S. ELIOT (b. 1888) may well dislike the word 'generation' since it tends to localise his poetry, level it down to the social criticism of a particular period of time. Certainly his work is rooted in the period in which it was written, but just as to know one man deeply is to have some knowledge of all men, so an exploration of one's own age must apply both to its past and its future. Eliot is a visionary poet, he is concerned with our human predicament, and that is comparatively unchanging behind its changing forms of expression. 'Disillusion', he is also chary about, because the word implies that there is no meaning to life, and Eliot certainly believes there is a meaning and that it is religious. Consequently there can only be 'the illusion of disillusion'. The meaning is to be found in man's relationship to God, and Eliot writes about this in terms which are far more specifically Christian than those of Wordsworth, Blake or Yeats. But like theirs his poetry is a bridge between the dimensions of time and eternity, flesh and spirit. It confirms an order of being about which we can have direct knowledge, but little information.

His work has an extremely logical progression and although it is customary to suggest a break between the statement of the 'Hollow Men' and that of 'Ash Wednesday', and link it to the poet's renewed affirmation of Anglo-Catholicism, all his poems have the same religious concern, even if the dynamic of the earlier ones is the futility of man when he is isolated from God and attempting to live by purely secular values.

Without a living *rapport* between the individual and his
God (it is certainly not appropriate to refer to our underlying
reality as the Unconscious when talking about Eliot's work)
there is stasis and impotency, since man is cut off from the
source and direction of his life. This is the impasse of J. Alfred
Prufrock, the first of the 'Hollow Men' who inhabit Eliot's
'Waste Land'. Prufrock is imprisoned in the guilt and complexities of his own ego. The title 'Love Song' is itself ironical since
he is cut off high and dry from instinct and passion, and incapable
of direct thought or spontaneous action.

> Should I, after tea and cakes and ices,
> Have the strength to force the moment to its crisis?
> But though I have wept and fasted, wept and prayed,
> Though I have seen my head (grown slightly bald) brought in
> > upon a platter,
> I am no prophet—and here's no great matter;
> I have seen the moment of my greatness flicker,
> And I have seen the eternal Footman hold my coat, and
> > snicker,
> And, in short, I was afraid.[1]

Psychologists suggest that anxiety is partly a question of unused
energy; certainly Prufrock, unable to use more than the minutest
part of himself, is hag-ridden by anxiety. Isolated from the heights
and depths of himself, he has become as circumscribed by the
immediate instant as the hands of a clock:

> For I have known them all already, known them all —
> Have known the evenings, mornings, afternoons,
> Have measured out my life with coffee spoons;

He longs to regress from his sterile self-consciousness into some
primitive marine beast; at least such a creature is rooted in its own
animality and so has purpose and direction.

> I should have been a pair of ragged claws
> Scuttling across the floors of silent seas.

[1] The Love Song of J. Alfred Prufrock.'

Only in fantasy is there any freedom; but there is nostalgia and beauty in Prufrock's dream of the sea-girls, those images of spontaneous life, which must be destroyed, for him, by the first breath of outer event:

> We have lingered in the chambers of the sea
> By sea-girls wreathed with seaweed red and brown
> Till human voices wake us, and we drown.

If we are out of touch with the 'spiritual ground' of ourselves then it is difficult to meet other people with any fulness. Since we only know the shadow of ourselves we can only know the shadow of our friends. Michael Hamburger ('The Unity of T. S. Eliot's Poetry', part of which appeared in *Envoy* Vol. 4. May–June 1959) has pointed out that the pathos of 'Portrait of a Lady' derives from the impossibility of communication, and of communion, between those whose lives are circumscribed by purely material ends. Eliot conveys the terrible incompatibility between the elderly lady and her young visitor by a characteristic juxtaposition of the tragic and the trivial:

> 'Ah, my friend, you do not know, you do not know
> What life is, you hold it in your hands';
> (Slowly twisting the lilac stalks)
> 'You let it flow from you, you let it flow,
> And youth is cruel, and has no remorse
> And smiles at situations which it cannot see.'
> I smile, of course,
> And go on drinking tea.[1]

These portraits are not merely satires on particular people, or a particular class. In the 'Rhapsody on a Windy Night' the imagery is not localised by any particular person but is general. After a night walk the poet returns at dawn to his own lodgings:

[1] 'Portrait of a Lady.'

The lamp said,
'Four o'clock,
Here is the number on the door.
Memory!
You have the key,
The little lamp spreads a ring on the stair,
Mount.
The bed is open; the tooth brush hangs on the wall,
Put your shoes at the door, sleep, prepare for life.'

The last twist of the knife.

Hamburger writes: 'the preparation for life—which is "the last twist of the knife", is the preparation for any life not sustained by a purpose which transcends that life; and the cruel finality of the last image conveys a despair so great that no material remedy could possibly prove effective.'

'Gerontion', the greatest inhabitant of the 'Waste Land', is not pathetic at all. In fact there is tragic grandeur, a whiff of salvation, about this old man whose destructive intellect explains away and rejects the Incarnation of Christ which intuitively he knows to be the meaning of existence:

Here I am, an old man in a dry month,
Being read to by a boy, waiting for rain.

Water and rain are symbols of the spirit. Like Prufrock, Gerontion has isolated himself against this creative force and so he is 'in the dry month' waiting for the rain which can never come, since he has rejected its origin.

From the point of view of analysis, this is perhaps Eliot's most difficult poem; some passages are of great complexity and ambiguity. But there is no mistaking the tragic personality which emerges from it. Gerontion becomes the type of every dying age and his decayed house is all Europe. With passionate rhetoric he analyses history, but analyses only to confuse the real issue which gives history its meaning, and which Eliot considers to be the birth of Christ. It is not only Gerontion but man himself who has

slowly withdrawn from his *raison d'être* and lost the very capacity
to feel in the process:

> I that was near your heart was removed therefrom
> To lose beauty in terror, terror in inquisition.
> I have lost my passion: why should I need to keep it
> Since what is kept must be adulterated?
> I have lost my sight, smell, hearing, taste and touch:
> How should I use them for your closer contact?

God has been rejected, so only time and the flesh seem to have
significance. In a fine passage Gerontion imagines himself and his
old friends blown outwards by death into oblivion:

> De Bailhacke, Fresca, Mrs. Cammel, whirled
> Beyond the circuit of the shuddering Bear
> In fractured atoms. Gull against the wind, in the windy straits
> Of Belle Isle, or running on the Horn,
> White feathers in the snow, the Gulf claims. . . .

'The Hollow Men' comes after 'The Waste Land'. I write about
it now because it seems to me the climax of Eliot's poems of
desolation. It is true that to 'the dead land' it opposes 'death's
dream kingdom', but although this suggests a life beyond death
which has more reality than earthly life, the tone of the poem is
one of rankling despair.

Its epigraph is 'Mistah Kurtz—he dead', the words which
announce the death of the protagonist of Conrad's short story,
'Heart of Darkness'. Kurtz had the energy and conviction at
least to be damned, but the lives of the 'Hollow Men' taste neither
of salvation nor damnation; only of futility:

> Our dried voices, when
> We whisper together
> Are quiet and meaningless
> As wind in dry grass
> Or rats' feet over broken glass
> In our dry cellar.

Because they have not dared to confront and understand themselves, these people have drifted through life like scraps of windblown paper, and after death they still wish to bypass such a meeting:

> Let me be no nearer
> In death's dream kingdom
> Let me also wear
> Such deliberate disguises
> Rat's coat, crowskin, crossed staves
> In a field
> Behaving as the wind behaves
> No nearer—
>
> Not that final meeting
> In the twilight kingdom.[1]

In 'The Waste Land' itself there is the same despair of the individual cut off from his spring of life, and abandoned to a treadmill of meaningless activity. But, far more clearly than in the preceding poems, we have brief hints and glimpses of the spiritual order which lies behind temporal existence. The poem wavers between the longing and half conviction which come from these flashes of insight and a sense of futility which is as bitter as 'The Hollow Men'. But the moments of vision are actual enough, despite the uncertainty, and in this sense the work presages the spiritual affirmation of 'Ash Wednesday'.

It is a religious poem concerned with the hopes and despair of man, rooted in time and material, and lost in the nightmare of separation and thirst:

> If there were water
> And no rock
> If there were rock
> And also water
> And water

[1] 'The Waste Land.'

A spring
A pool among the rock
If there were the sound of water only
Not the cicada
And dry grass singing
But sound of water over rock
Where the hermit-thrush sings in the pine trees
Drip drop drip drop drop drop drop
But there is no water.

The short broken lines communicate both frustration and longing. 'The Waste Land', however, is not wholly a desert. Signs—ambiguous and difficult to interpret but unavoidable— show it is overshadowed by another reality whose significance is not material:

Who is the third who walks always beside you?
When I count, there are only you and I together
But when I look ahead up the white road
There is always another one walking beside you
Gliding wrapt in a brown mantle, hooded
I do not know whether a man or a woman
But who is that on the other side of you?

Eliot says these lines were stimulated by the account of Shackleton's experience in an Antarctic expedition. At the extremity of their strength, the explorers had the conviction that there was another member of their party, invisible but present to them all. When climbing alone on Everest, Smythe sensed a similar mysterious stranger; in fact this unknown companion seems a frequent experience of people in great isolation and exhaustion. The lines also hint at Christ on the road to Emmaus; the point is that the inexplicable revelation cannot be explained away. It is as much a part of 'The Waste Land' as the Hotel Metropole, though ignored by those of its inhabitants who are wedded to brute fact, Sweeney for example, or Mrs. Porter.

The land is waste because its inhabitants seem to have lost contact with the divine powers which should nourish it. The images of religion and myth are a language of these powers, but meaning has seeped out of them until they are only—

A heap of broken images, where the sun beats . . . .

Without a forthright communion between God and man, human life is sterile, and this affects the central fertility rite of marriage. In 'The Game of Chess' section of the poem, sex is divested of its romantic glamour and shown as a bitter hysterical conflict between man and woman. Because we are out of touch with the heights and depths of ourselves we cannot meet each other,

'My nerves are bad tonight. Yes, bad. Stay with me.
'Speak to me. Why do you never speak. Speak.
'What are you thinking of? What thinking? What?
'I never know what you are thinking. Think.'

It is the whole of society which has suffered this dislocation. While the rich are cut off from each other in the cages of their anxiety and self-consciousness, the poor are coarsened by the animality which dominates their lives:

You ought to be ashamed, I said, to look so antique.
(And her only thirty-one.)
I can't help it, she said, pulling a long face,
It's them pills I took, to bring it off, she said.
(She's had five already, and nearly died of young George.)
The chemist said it would be all right, but I've never been the
                                                        same.
You *are* a proper fool, I said.
Well, if Albert wont leave you alone, there it is, I said,
What you get married for if you don't want children?
HURRY UP PLEASE IT'S TIME

This public house conversation with its hint of abortion, the offence against life itself, is the nadir of materialism. But the barman's refrain 'Hurry Up Please It's Time' suggests death and so sets it in the context of eternity. The drinkers are unaware of this, but their time no more circumscribes them than their bodies. By making their beery good-nights change into the farewell of the mad and doomed Ophelia, Eliot restores to them the pathos of their actual but forgotten situation, the duality of flesh and spirit.

Good night ladies, good night, sweet ladies, good night, good night.

The third section takes its title from the Fire Sermon of the Buddha. Gautama tells the assembled priests that all things are on fire. 'And with what are they on fire?' ask the priests. The Buddha replies, 'With the fire of passion, with the fire of hatred, with the fire of infatuation; with birth, old age, death, sorrow, misery and despair are they on fire.'

The way of the disciple is to turn from the world and become free of attachment. This fire of time fixated longing which involves us in repetitive sexuality, and the escape from it, is the theme of this section of the poem. Tiresias, the seer, watches with detachment those who are involved with the burning wheel. There is the typist who couples with her carbuncular lover, but with complete indifference:

> She turns and looks a moment in the glass,
> Hardly aware of her departed lover;
> Her brain allows one half formed thought to pass:
> 'Well now that's done: and I'm glad it's over.'

The Thames daughters are caught up in the same reiterated action which has no meaning since it is divorced from understanding and love:

> 'Trams and dusty trees.
> Highbury bore me. Richmond and Kew
> Undid me. By Richmond I raised my knees
> Supine on the floor of a narrow canoe.'

The 'Fire Sermon' section closes with echoes of the Buddha and St. Augustine, two great teachers who show the way from

the Wheel of Ignorance and Fantasy. It also ends with a line from
the Mass, 'O Lord Thou pluckest me out,' the broken prayer of
the penitent that he may be a brand plucked from the burning.

The short poem, 'Death by Water', with its beautiful swaying
rhythm suggests not only physical death by drowning, but the
death in life, with its possibility of rebirth, which is associated
with baptism. This theme is taken up at the start of the final
poem, 'What the Thunder Said', which evokes all those gods
who must die in order to be reborn and then relates them to our
present situation:

> After the torchlight red on sweaty faces
> After the frosty silence in the gardens
> After the agony in stony places
> The shouting and the crying
> Prison and palace and reverberation
> Of thunder of spring over distant mountains
> He who was living is now dead
> We who were living are now dying
> With a little patience

This last poem has an apocalyptic quality about it, as if the
death in life which every one of us should undergo, implies the
end of civilisation:

> Who are these hooded hordes swarming
> Over endless plains, stumbling in cracked earth
> Ringed by the flat horizon only
> What is the city over the mountains
> Cracks and reforms and bursts in the violet air
> Falling towers
> Jerusalem Athens Alexandria
> Vienna London
> Unreal

The individual is still imprisoned within his own small ego, but at
least there are possibilities of escape:

I have heard the key
Turn in the door once and turn once only
We think of the key, each in his prison
Thinking of the key, each confirms a prison
Only at nightfall, aethereal rumours
Revive for a moment a broken Coriolanus

The poem ends with the repetition of the word 'Shantih' which Eliot tells us in a note is a formal ending to a Upanishad; 'The peace which passeth understanding,' is our equivalent of the word.' But this word of resolution is preceded by disjointed fragments, 'London Bridge is falling down. . . . O swallow, swallow. . . . Hiernonymo's mad again'. They express the desperation, and wavering between doubt and faith, resolution and chaos, which runs through the poem. However, the conclusion at least hints at a way out of the Waste Land.

This is, at first reading, a confusing poem. One becomes lost in the wealth of mythical images and the quotations from many literatures. Some of the links between passages have been cut and it is necessary to pass these gaps by a leap of the imagination. Nevertheless such criticisms are largely irrelevant. 'The Waste Land' involves both the heart and mind in its exploration of our human condition. This, I suspect, is the job it is supposed to do and it is an effective poem.

Eliot prefaces his dramatic fragment, 'Sweeney Agonistes', with a quotation from St. John of the Cross, 'Hence the soul cannot be possessed of the divine union until it has divested itself of the love of created beings.' Now most visionary poets are involved with this divine union, but they seek it not by negation, rather by a celebration of life in all its varied forms. God is the source of all which truly lives, and everything which lives is in some sense a metaphor of God. The poet himself has the same reality and so he needs neither affirmation or denial.

Such a 'yes saying' to life is more usual to poets than Eliot's attempt to seek communion with God, not through his creation, but beyond it. He is, in some of his poems, a mystic of the negative way, and 'Ash Wednesday' is a poem of the soul's withdrawal. It tells of the willed surrender of the personality, with its earthbound needs, to a central and divine experience. The deprivation is willingly accepted, so it is no longer sterile. There has been at least some inkling of the redeeming vision, and although the desert of 'The Waste Land' remains, it blends with images of the rose and the garden, which suggest that the new life of the spirit comes out of dryness and the death of the 'old man' with his time-fixated desires:

> The single Rose
> Is now the Garden
> Where all loves end. . . .
> Grace to the Mother
> For the Garden
> Where all love ends.

Death is no longer associated with symbols of corruption, the rat, the cellar and the lipless grin of earlier poems, but with the Mother, since once there has been a vision beyond mortality Death becomes the matrix of new growth and renewal.

'Ash Wednesday' is about the journey of the soul and the dangers which beset it. This is the theme of many religious writers, of the anonymous authors of fairy stories and myths, and perhaps of Homer's Odyssey. Eliot uses the traditional image of the Stair and fragments of the Liturgy of the Mass to suggest the slow and difficult journey of the soul through its own doubts and illusions towards some partial realisation of God:

> Distraction, music of the flute, stops and steps of the mind
>   over the third stair,
> Fading, fading; strength beyond hope and despair
> Climbing the third stair.

> Lord, I am not worthy
> Lord, I am not worthy
>   but speak the word only.

There must always be conflict between our longing for the sensory world and the demands of the spirit:

And the lost heart stiffens and rejoices
In the lost lilac and the lost sea voices
And the weak spirit quickens to rebel
For the bent golden-rod and the lost sea smell
Quickens to recover
The cry of quail and the whirling plover
And the blind eye creates
The empty forms between the ivory gates
And smell renews the salt savour of the sandy earth.

While we are involved in time and space there will never be a complete solution of this conflict, but there is at least discipline, penitence, patience and the realisation that carnal love is the imperfect expression of a longing whose true goal and satisfaction must be sought in God:

> Teach us to sit still
> Even among these rocks,
> Our peace is His will
> And even among these rocks
> Sister, mother
> And spirit of the river, spirit of the sea,
> Suffer me not to be separated
>
> And let my cry come unto Thee.

The 'Four Quartets' are concerned with Eliot's mystical experience, and like all mystics, he questions the ability of language to convey it. 'The poetry,' he writes in 'East Coker', 'does not matter', as if words had become less important than the experience they strive to convey:

> The dove descending breaks the air
> With flame of incandescent terror. . . .[1]

The pentecostal moments exist when we are aware of a dimension which is not subject to time or space, and the warring

[1] 'Little Gidding.'

opposites of life reach some brief harmony. But they come to us out of darkness and must be prepared for by the deprivation of sense and the surrender of hope.

> I said to my soul, be still, and let the dark come upon you
> Which shall be the darkness of God. . . .
> I said to my soul, be still, and wait without hope
> For hope would be hope for the wrong thing; wait without
> love
> For love would be love of the wrong thing; there is yet
> faith
> But the faith and the love and the hope are all in the waiting.
> Wait without thought, for you are not ready for thought:
> So the darkness shall be the light, and the stillness the dancing.[1]

The 'Four Quartets' are not poems of escape from the temporal world. They attempt to show how it is crossed and given meaning by the eternal:

> 'The point of intersection of the timeless
> With time . . . .'

It is no longer a question, as it was in the earlier poems, of matter cancelling out spirit, but of their mutual interaction and fruitfulness:

> Whisper of running streams, and winter lightning,
> The wild thyme unseen and the wild strawberry,
> The laughter in the garden, echoed ecstasy
> Not lost, but requiring, pointing to the agony
> Of death and birth.

Eliot has reached a point where he no longer sees the garden, flower and stream as deceptions, since these images participate in eternity. It is the double vision, and in it human love is accepted and affirmed, though as a beginning, not an end in itself:[2]

[1] 'East Coker.'
[2] See the essay—already quoted on p. 52—by Michael Hamburger.

—not less of love but expanding
Of love beyond desire, and so liberation
From the future as well as the past.[1]

It is not a question of avoiding experience but of realising that
our experience in time has a meaning beyond time, that conflict
and the unravelling of our complexities and darkness are the
growing pains of the spirit:

> The wounded surgeon plies the steel
> That questions the distempered part;
> Beneath the bleeding hands we feel
> The sharp compassion of the healer's art
> Resolving the enigma of the fever chart.

Human animality, 'substantial flesh and blood', wishes to deny
this, but the fact remains that simply by being born and involved
in human life we must perforce experience something analogous
to the Crucifixion and realise, however unwillingly, that it is
good:

> The dripping blood our only drink,
> The bloody flesh our only food:
> In spite of which we like to think
> That we are sound, substantial flesh and blood—
> Again, in spite of that, we call this Friday good.[2]

'The Waste Land' hinted at a spiritual direction to life and
it was the way out of the cage of barren individuality. The
'Four Quartets' tell us more about this way. In sudden sparks of
insight the human being is realised both as a process and its
cause, the single illuminated instant comprehending both our
end and our beginning. It is not possible to sustain here these all-
encompassing moments, but the fact remains that they give this
life its meaning, and to the individual the patience to endure the

[1] 'Little Gidding.'
[2] 'East Coker.'

contradictions of existence. In his poetry Eliot has explored the
fallen condition of the soul, and re-affirmed the way of liberation:

> We must be still and still moving
> Into another intensity
> For a further union, a deeper communion
> Through the dark cold and the empty desolation,
> The wave cry, the wind cry, the vast waters
> Of the petrel and the porpoise. In my end is my beginning.

E

5

Ezra Pound — Edwin Muir — Edith Sitwell — Robert Graves — Kathleen Raine

As an American poet Ezra Pound (b. 1885) should be outside the scope of this book, but his work is too much a part of the landscape of contemporary English Verse to be ignored. I remember Robert Frost on his last visit to England talking about him. 'Poets,' he said 'get plugged into terminals, electric terminals, and the terminal that Ezra's got himself hitched into is a mighty black one. They come over to talk to him, the intelligentsia, and he tells them about the purity of the American race, and Jews and Blacks, and all that stuff and they take it down in their little note-books for working up into a thesis.' Then Frost roared with laughter, 'The purity of the American Race,' he chanted, 'purity. . . !'

Now, as I said before, poets are not making pretty patterns with words, but statements which bear either a true or false reference to man himself or his environment. If they are merely busy with pretty patterns or drooling gently about sheep and cows their work will quite rightly be dumped into the dustbin of literature. But what if they are making assertions, but those assertions are patently false? Is it possible, for instance, to think of an ode celebrating with joy the massacres of Belsen and Dachau, and for it to be great poetry?

Obviously no generation has a monopoly of truth, but I suggest that it is possible to have at least an intuitive awareness of truth's trend and moral direction, and that if a poem deviates from this direction then it will be bad art, and have at best only a rather feverish case-book interest. I think this applies to much of Pound's work. This extract from 'The Cantos', for instance, seems to ignore so much of the complexity and tragedy of the

66

human situation as to be patently false. Whatever interest it has, comes from the revelation of a state of mind. But that state of mind is so enclosed by personal hatred that its significance is purely clinical:

> S . . . t on the throne of England, s . . t on the Austrian sofa,
> In their souls was usura and in their minds darkness
> and blankness, greased fat were four Georges
> Pus was in Spain, Wellington was a jew's pimp
> and lacked mind to know what he effected.
> 'Leave the Duke, go for gold!'
> In their souls was usura and in their hearts cowardice,
> In their minds was stink and corruption.
> Two sores ran together, Talleyrand stank with shanker,
> and hell pissed up Metternich.
> Filth stank as in our day.

But Ezra Pound is occasionally a poet and at times gives us passages of great significance and beauty:

> The ant's a centaur in his dragon world.
> Pull down thy vanity, it is not man
> Made courage, or made order, or made grace,
> Pull down thy vanity, I say pull down.
> Learn of the green world what can be thy place
> In scaled invention or true artistry,
> Pull down thy vanity,
>   Paquin pull down!
> The green casque has outdone your elegance.
>
> 'Master thyself, then others shall thee beare'
> Pull down thy vanity
> Thou art a beaten dog beneath the hail,
> A swollen magpie in a fitful sun,
> Half black half white
> Nor knowst'ou wing from tail
> Pull down thy vanity. . . .[1]

[1] 'Pisan Cantos.'

Perhaps to say Pound is plugged into a terminal and it is black, suggests a definite intention and atmosphere to his work which I have never found. All-embracing the Cantos certainly are; but I do not mean by this they have the universality of great poetry, but that he has crammed into the enormous rag-bag of this work every thought and scrap of information which ever came his way. The poet's ego seems to have abnegated its critical and selective task; the cold, seeing eye of Odin has gone, so almost 'anything goes'. We find a few lines of Confucius, for example, and a quotation from a Stock Exchange Directory, sandwiched between a growl of the purest paranoia, and one or two phrases of splendid lyricism. Reading 'The Cantos' is like wandering through the ruins of a great city in a fog. Birds and ghosts cackle or flute melodiously from crumbling walls. The mist lifts for an instant and one sees a bronze lynx beside a very fine example of an antique cistern. Then visibility fails again, and one is crawling on hands and knees over a mess that was once undoubtedly the city midden. Interesting objects abound and there are many old hieroglyphics for antiquarians to decipher. There are also brief glimpses of a dazzling archaic landscape for lovers of beauty. But although one can spend a very industrious and enjoyable day picking about among the Cantos, I am not at all sure that they bear much resemblance to great poetry.

There is much that is dark and turgid in Pound's work despite the moments of illumination, but the atmosphere of Edwin Muir's poetry (1887–1959) is one of charity and light. Too charitable and too light, one tends to mutter, after reading through poem after impeccable poem in which the worthiest sentiments are expressed in beautiful but rather tired language:

> Reality or vision, this we have seen.
> If it had lasted but another moment
> It might have held for ever! But the world
> Rolled back into its place, and we are here,
> And all that radiant kingdom lies forlorn,
> As if it had never stirred: no human voice

Is heard among the meadows, but it speaks
To itself alone, alone it flowers and shines
And blossoms for itself while time runs on.[1]

'The Transfiguration' expresses, with reference to Christ upon the mountain, the visionary moment which gathers up, and seems to resolve within itself, all the oppositions of temporal life. The trouble with such verse is that although it has no doubt been distilled out of conflict, it seems in the distilling process to have shed the essence of life. I have no doubt Muir's experience was real, but the lines I quote—and this seems to me true of very many of his poems—do not communicate this reality. They describe it, are diagrams which give us some impression of it, but they do not recreate it for us within the language itself. Probably a great many of Muir's poems lack the energy needed for permanence. But some of them have this power, and since his themes are central to visionary poetry, these few poems are of great significance. Muir has the double vision and sees our mortal life as overshadowed by a timeless world. In many of his poems he uses myths and fables because every human being is in some sense a character of myth, his life a fable. The aim is to:

> Seek the beginnings, learn from whence you came,
> And know the various earths of which you are made . . . .

One must enter into the labyrinth of oneself and patiently decipher all the living complexities whether of the past or future:

> I must in other lives with many a leap
> Blindfold, must lodge in dark and narrow skulls
> With a few thoughts that pad from wall to wall
> And never get out, must moulder in dusty hearts,
> Inhabit many a dark or sunny room,
> Be in all things.[2]

The maze of the past in which we are implicated is the past of all mankind. The object of living is to seek a way out towards the

[1] 'The Transfiguration.' From *The Collected Poems of Edwin Muir.*
[2] 'The Journey Back.'

light and find the 'drowned original of the soul'. In many of his poems Muir writes with wisdom and clarity. In some of them he breaks through the time barrier, in 'The Child Dying' for instance, which I quote in full:

Unfriendly friendly universe,
I pack your stars into my purse,
And bid you, bid you so farewell.
That I can leave you, quite go out,
Go out, go out beyond all doubt,
My father says, is the miracle.

You are so great, and I so small:
I am nothing, you are all:
Being nothing, I can take this way.
Oh I need neither rise nor fall,
For when I do not move at all
I shall be out of all your day.

It's said some memory will remain
In the other place, grass in the rain,
Light on the land, sun on the sea,
A flitting grace, a phantom face,
But the world is out. There is no place
Where it and its ghost can ever be.

Father, father, I dread this air
Blown from the far side of despair,
The cold cold corner. What house, what hold,
What hand is there? I look and see
Nothing-filled eternity,
And the great round world grows weak and old

Hold my hand, Oh hold it fast—
I am changing!—until at last
My hand in yours no more will change,
Though yours change on. You here, I there,
So hand in hand, twin-leafed despair—
I did not know death was so strange.

I certainly would not agree with the critic who said the achievement of Dame Edith Sitwell (b. 1887) was in the realm of publicity rather than of letters, but there is an edge of truth to the gibe. A lifelong concern with verse may affect the personality, but it is the verse which matters, not the poet's eye in a fine frenzy rolling, or the floating hair. It is not that Dame Edith wears her singing robes a trifle flamboyantly but that her verse itself often has a theatrical flavour. At times she seems to be fishing up highly coloured images from the chest of English Literature in order to deck herself for a charade in which she plays the heroine.

Ostensibly much of her later verse is about events of extreme and tragic importance. 'The Shadow of Cain' deals with the dropping of atomic bombs on Hiroshima and Nagasaki, but this poem is so weighed down with portentous symbolism that the horror of those events is crowded out. Of course great images are a quality of poetry, but if the last farthing has not been paid for them in terms of personal suffering, then they will not be an organic quality of the work, but draped or pinned about it for decoration. I feel this is very often the case with Edith Sitwell's verse. At first one is delighted by her world of amber dust, dark leaved arbutus blooms, lions and skeletons. But after further reading one gets a sense of being let down, as if her poems were often elaborate façades with nothing behind them, traps which catch little but themselves. They seem to me to lack the grit and sweat of real experience which makes sense of the rhetoric of Yeats or Dylan Thomas. Both these poets are 'personalities' but the personality is subordinate to the verse. With Edith Sitwell the verse often seems to feed the personality, to be decor for a personal gesture.

Certainly Yeats could make such gestures, as in the conclusion to 'High Talk':

> All metaphor, Malachi, stilts and all. A barnacle goose
> Far up in the stretches of night; night splits and the dawn breaks
> loose;
> I, through the terrible novelty of light, stalk on, stalk on;
> Those great sea-horses bare their teeth and laugh at the dawn.

Here the poet introduces himself into the landscape 'I through the terrible novelty of light, stalk on, stalk on . . .'. But by some subtle nuance of the language (it is partly the force of the verb, stalk) he dehumanises himself so that we do not think of Mr. Willie Yeats taking a picturesque walk along the beach, but of man himself as part of the immense light-washed processes of nature. He has become in this poem both greater and less than himself, and though, by all accounts, Yeats was not a humble man, one cannot separate character from the verse, and this effect depends on humility.

At the beginning of her poem, 'The Coat of Fire', Dame Edith Sitwell is also taking a walk, not, however, along a particular beach or cliff-top, but in a vague and nightmarish landscape, which is like Hell, since she believes the contemporary human situation savours of the infernal. She is a pillar of fire and she walks through darkness and fog along hard, black, marble pavements. The vitality of these somewhat incompatible images is undeniable, but it seems directed on the poet herself, somewhat in the manner of limelight, rather than any general human predicament.

In the passage from Yeats, sea, sky, bird, light and the poet himself all seem parts of a movement which comprehends but exceeds them. In this verse of Edith Sitwell the emphasis is upon 'I'. Thunder, darkness, fog and the pavement·of hell, these are properties, and used not to further an apocalyptic vision which includes the poet, but to aggrandise her persona, the pillar of fire.

Again in 'A Hymn to Venus', an old woman kneels before the sea and prays to the goddess. The poem is partly a lamentation for past youth. It also suggests that consolation may be found for the mutability of the flesh and erotic love by considering the mutations of the physical body in which our spiritual being is clothed.

The verse is studded with such great traditional counters of poetry as the rose, the rainbow, the ruby, dew, eternity. Both Yeats and Eliot have shown that these ancient images are still valid for poetry, but Dame Edith seems not so much to make statements with them as to linger tenderly on their sound value and pictorial glamour. Taking the poem as a whole, she does not seem to have put the energy of her own thought and feeling behind the words.

In the poem of Yeats a real sea is evoked by the personification of the horses which 'bare their teeth and laugh at the dawn'. In 'A Hymn to Venus', however, the importance of the sea does not seem to lie within itself, but in the poet who is kneeling beside it. The effect of such verse is that of a pageant, and at first one is ready to applaud the actor in her colourful robes and tragic mask. But after a while the atmosphere becomes extremely stuffy, perhaps because the whole performance is enclosed within the ego; a very small theatre.

This criticism could apply to much of the later verse of Edith Sitwell. But in some of her work, particularly of an earlier period, she expresses a savage desolation which is both moving and completely sincere. In 'Gold Coast Customs' she expresses a fierce indignation at materialism and exploitation, and because the violent images of this poem, and its extraordinary range of sound serve this purpose, we are involved, not in a colourful entertainment but a profound comment on a facet of human existence.

I would have liked to quote in full a poem called 'Lullaby', but unfortunately Dame Edith has refused to allow the publishers to reproduce any of her poetry in this book. One can say, however, that this poem expresses with extreme economy—there is no reaching after effect or brilliant pyrotechnics—the desolation and pathos of the human spirit, confronted by those forces which are destructive and against life, although we ourselves have created them. I can think of scarcely another poem which evokes so powerfully this situation of our present age.

In this poem Edith Sitwell has surrendered to the experience, and not used it to create a flattering picture of herself. Inspiration takes over the job, and so there is no sense of muscles being strained in order 'to knock them cold'; she has written many poems of a similar quality, but one wonders why she so often subordinates the 'Muse' to her own personality.

Of all living poets of high reputation, Robert Graves (b. 1895) was perhaps one of the most widely represented in the Poetry Bookshop anthologies edited by Harold Monro. It is easy to see why. Very many of his early poems have just the muted note, the blend of countryside observation and harmless, charming fancy

which would have endeared them to the Georgian appetite.
'An English Wood' for instance, is as undisturbing and pleasant
as a watercolour by someone's maiden aunt!

> Only, the lawns are soft,
> The tree-stems grave and old;
> Slow branches sway aloft,
> The evening air comes cold,
> The sunset scatters gold.
> Small grasses toss and bend,
> Small pathways idly tend
> Towards no fearful end.

Then there is the note of 'faerie'. In this vein Graves can write as
whimsically as Walter de la Mare in his most relaxed mood;
and that is saying a great deal. Here is the beginning of 'The
Bedpost':

> Sleepy Betsy from her pillow
> Sees the post and ball
> Of her sister's wooden bedstead
> Shadowed on the wall.

> Now this grave young warror standing
> With uncovered head
> Tells her stories of old battle
> As she lies in bed:

So far so good, but what are the stories about?

> How the daughters of the Emperor,
> Diving boldly through
> Caught and killed their father's murderer,
> Old Cro-bar-cru.

> How the Farmer's sturdy sons
> Fought the Giant Gog,
> Threw him into Stony Cataract
> In the land of Og.

Fairy tales are a folk psychology and at their best describe nothing less than the wanderings and dangers of the human soul on its journey. I have as strong a stomach for them as the next man, but it certainly turns at *Old Cro-bar-cru* or the *Giant Gog*, and *Og*. I suppose they could be defended as scholarly jokes, relaxed and whimsical, but to me they seem dangerously close to those plaster gnomes with red painted caps, fishing rods and attendant bunny rabbits.

Like the W. J. Turner of 'Chimborazo and Cotopaxi', Graves makes us 'free of the kingdom of faerie, or poesie'; the terms are interchangeable.

> Could I make it so that you
> Might wonder at them too!
> Glories of land and sea,
> Of Heaven glittering free,
> Castles hugely built in Spain,
> Glories of Cockaigne,
> Of that spicy kingdom, Cand,
> Of the Delectable Land,
> Of the Land of Crooked Stiles
> Of the Fortunate Isles.[1]

And so on. It is true that the final point of this poem is to contrast these fancies with the dull flatness of Hell. But Hell seems tagged on as an afterthought; for intensity of realisation, the kingdom of sugar and spice wins hands down.

Then there are poems like 'Love in Barreness'; pleasing gestures to the Romantic Situation but with no particular force or edge to lift them from the ruck of amorous verse:

> The North Wind rose: I saw him press
> With lusty force against your dress,
> Moulding your body's inward grace
> And streaming off from your set face;

[1] 'In Procession.'

So now no longer flesh and blood
But poised in marble flight you stood.
O Wingless Victory, loved of men,
Who could withstand your beauty then?[1]

This is very much the conventional romantic exercise, a set
piece whose object is itself, not a woman.

Green hills of May, ornamental piskies and lovely ladies care-
less and gay, there are such platitudes in the early work of Graves.
But even in the earlier poems something begins to use the
romantic furniture which has nothing to do with 'poesie'. In
'Apples and Water', a girl watches the parched soldiers stamping
by and wishes to quench their thirst. But her mother tells her:

> 'There is no water can supply them
> In western streams that flow;
> There is no fruit can satisfy them
> On orchard-trees that grow.
>
> 'Once in my youth I gave, poor fool,
> A soldier apples and water:
> And may I die before you cool
> Such drouth as his, my daughter.'

Here fairy story is used not to create a 'fay' atmosphere, but to
illuminate a situation of real life. We know this thirst and we
know it is unquenchable, consequently the poem is honest
because it is making a referential statement; it tells us something
about our human need and its insatiability. Again in a poem like
'Ancestors', at first one feels this is a pleasant, half-humorous
evocation of the shades of the past,

> My New Year's drink is mulled tonight
> And hot sweet vapours roofward twine.
> The shades cry *Gloria!* with delight
> As down they troop to taste old wine.

[1] 'Love in Barrenness.'

But the last two verses wipe the playful smile off the poem. The shades are not genial, old topers, but the backwash of past time, lost souls who wish to involve us in their own disintegration:

> I watch their brightening boastful eyes,
> I hear the toast their glasses clink:
> 'May this young man in drink grown wise
> Die, as we also died, in drink!'
>
> Their reedy voices I abhor,
> I am alive at least, and young.
> I dash their swill upon the floor:
> Let them lap grovelling, tongue to tongue.

One finds in the poems of Robert Graves a steady increase of the sense of reality, and now their climate and landscape is about as inhospitable to a little man with a red cap as the summit of the Matterhorn.

Perhaps no living poet has expressed with such understanding and immediacy the meeting between man and woman. By immediacy I do not mean that his poems are *cris de coeur*; the fact that they express accurately a human situation, implies 'The Watcher', that is to say some element of the self which remains detached and critical. But there is a sense of exposure, of the poet having opened himself to the full force of life, and that life has gone through him into the poem. One feels in very many of Graves's later poems that he has paid the *last farthing* for their experience and consequently can communicate it without rhetoric or ornament, but with telling accuracy. The final image of 'Spoils', for example, brings home with an almost physical impact the inescapability of profound feeling:

> The spoils of love present a different case,
> When all is over and you march for home:
> That lock of hair, these letters and the portrait
> May not be publicly displayed; nor sold;
> Nor burned; nor returned (the heart being obstinate)—
> Yet never dare entrust them to a safe
> For fear they burn a hole through two-foot steel.

In a poem like 'Counting the Beats', Graves almost dispenses
with metaphor. It is concerned with the relationship of a man
and woman, who are in time and in love, to a process which is
both timeless and impersonal. I suppose a convenient label for it
is eternity. That Graves can express this conflict with such
economy and strength is a measure of his poetic development,
and the very great importance of his work:

> You, love, and I,
> (He whispers) you and I,
> And if no more than only you and I
> What care you or I?

> Counting the beats,
> Counting the slow heart beats,
> The bleeding to death of time in slow heart beats,
> Wakeful they lie.

> Cloudless day,
> Night, and a cloudless day;
> Yet the huge storm will burst upon their heads one day
> From a bitter sky.

> Where shall we be,
> (She whispers) where shall we be,
> When death strikes home, O where then shall we be
> Who were you and I?

> Not there but here,
> (He whispers) only here,
> As we are, here, together, now and here,
> Always you and I.

> Counting the beats,
> Counting the slow heart beats,
> The bleeding to death of time in slow heart beats,
> Wakeful they lie.

Much that I have said about Edwin Muir applies to Kathleen Raine (b. 1909), a visionary poet, whose work, at times, lacks the substance which is necessary for poetry, and goes over into the thin, diagrammatic language which is characteristic of much mystical writing.

> It burns in the void
> Nothing upholds it.
> Still it travels.
>
> Travelling the void
> Upheld by burning
> Nothing is still.
>
> Burning it travels.
> The void upholds it.
> Still it is nothing.
>
> Nothing it travels
> A burning void
> Upheld by stillness.[1]

It is very difficult to treat as directly as this of the Divine Original which sustains all life, and make it vital in the language of a poem. Perhaps by its very nature, Kathleen Raine is writing here *about* her theme, making a chart of it with a few brief lines. The verse is a pointer towards an important experience, but it does not create that experience within itself. What is perhaps unique about Kathleen Raine's work is her ability to create a kind of incantation or spell, which is reminiscent of the bardic poetry of Ireland and some ancient folk tales. In this vein there is nothing thin or diagrammatic about her verse, in fact it has an almost functional directness, which reminds us of the magical origins of poetry, its use to curse or bless, and bring success in battle.

> God in me is the fury on the bare heath
> God in me shakes the interior kingdom of my heaven.
> God in me is the fire wherein I burn.

[1] 'The World.' *Collected Poems.*

God in me swirling cloud and driving rain
God in me cries a lonely nameless bird
God in me beats my head upon a stone.

God in me the four elements of storm
Raging in the shelterless landscape of the mind
Outside the barred doors of my Goneril heart.[1]

[1] 'Storm.' *Collected Poems.*

6

A Note on the Thirties

THE PRIMARY concern of all the poets I have talked about so far is man himself. Of course you cannot separate a human being from his environment: they are as inter-related as the body and mind. But for Yeats, Eliot, Muir, Robert Graves and Edith Sitwell, human life is a spiritual process and consequently, although conditioned by external and material influences, man's destiny can finally only be understood by con-sidering man himself. That Self is the dynamic of history and its exploration is a task of visionary poetry.

In the Thirties there was a reaction against this standpoint. Not that the poets of this period were simple enough to take over the cruder fantasies of popular science and think that a dog could be wagged by his tail, and a human being completely conditioned by the cells of his body and food supply. But just as an adolescent is often impatient with a religious interpretation of life because it seems to fob off his immediate problems, sex for instance, or the business of earning a living, so the poets of the Thirties were suspicious of the subjective, religious approach. It obscured social evil.

Certainly, in this period evil had a peculiar clarity and external urgency. At home it walked with the hunger marchers and hovered over the unemployed at their street corners.

> In railway halls, on pavements near the traffic
> They beg, their eyes made big by empty staring
> And only measuring Time like the blank clock.
>
> No I shall weave no tracery of pen ornament
> To make them birds upon my singing tree
> Time merely drives these lives that do not live
> As tides push rotten stuff along the shore.[1]

[1] STEPHEN SPENDER: In Railway Halls.

Abroad, evil was the gathering violence of Nazism and Fascism, and so appalling and close was its contemporary expression that its eternal, subjective significance had to be shelved. It is no wonder poets like Auden, Day Lewis and Spender felt they must use their art almost as propaganda to thwart these inhuman forces.

> Tomorrow the rediscovery of romantic love
> The photographing of ravens, all the fun under
> Liberty's masterful shadow
>   . . . but today the struggle.
> Today the makeshift consolation; the shared cigarette.
> The cards in the candlelit barn and the scraping concert,
> The masculine jokes; today the
> Fumbled and unsatisfactory embrace before hurting.
> The stars are dead, the animals will not look:
> We are left alone with our day and the time is short and
> History to the defeated
> May say Alas but cannot help or pardon.[1]

If we tend nowadays to think of Auden's 'Spain' as a trifle stark, we must remember that its concluding statement—at least as far as our recent history is concerned—is probably true. Certainly the shadows of Fascism and economic exploitation over this period made it inevitable that poets should often write as if wickedness was not so much a perennial condition of every human heart which we must all personally deal with, as outside, in the Capitalists and the jack-booted S.S. men. Thus when David Gascoyne writes about the Crucifixion, we are the callous spectators of the torture of God, not the executioners of the divine principle within ourselves. Both views are true, but the climate of the Thirties made it unavoidable that poets should stress the external one:

> He is suspended on the cross tree now
> And we are onlookers at the crime,
> Callous contemporaries of the slow
> Torture of God. Here is the hill
> Made ghastly by his spattered blood.

[1] W. H. AUDEN: *Spain*.

Whereon He hangs and suffers still;
See, the centurions wear riding boots,
Black shirts and badges and peaked caps
Greet one another with raised-arm salutes;
They have cold eyes, unsmiling lips;
Yet these his brothers know not what they do.

And on his either side hang dead
A labourer or a factory hand
Or one is maybe a lynched Jew
And one a Negro or a Red,
Coolie or Ethiopian, Irishman,
Spaniard or German Democrat.[1]

There was an obviousness about the wickedness of the Thirties
which called for instant action, and made poets point their work
at it like an accusing finger or a gun. And just as evil could be seen
rampaging outside the individual, like Picasso's Minotaur, so
good also had its external form in those days, though with far
less objective justification: the Soviet Union became the great,
white place where justice was done, and if we shrug our shoulders
at the post-war about turn of Spender and Auden we must
remember that after the French Revolution Wordsworth
experienced a similar disillusion with France and her dictatorship.
    Certainly there was a severe deflation after the war. Nazism
was at least superficially destroyed on the continent, and at
home there was a considerably greater degree of social justice;
but there was no millenium. The Commissars had become re-
markably like the capitalists, and Russia had lost her holy glow
and become just another grey beast in the European jungle. I
think this poem of Roy Fuller expresses the situation:

When the hero's task was done
And the beast lay underground,
In the time that he had won
From the fates that pushed him round

[1] 'Ecce Homo.'

83

He had space to contemplate
How the peasants still were bled
And that in the salvaged state
Worms continued at the head.

Little space: already, where
Sweetly he enjoyed his fish,
Seeing through the shouldered hair
Loosening sails and dirty dish,

Gasped a pale new plea for aid.
Cleaning his gun later, he
Felt with awe the old beast's shade
Fall across the wine dark sea.[1]

The war, no doubt was necessary, but evil had not been destroyed by it, intangible as the air we breathe, it was as inescapable. It is of course quite inaccurate to think of the poets of the Thirties as simply concerned with politics, but there was an unusually out-turned direction to their work, and a sense that human conflict could reach a universal and fairly acceptable solution by some change in the order of society. Such an illusion has disappeared now, and once more the emphasis is on man himself; that is where good and evil start and their true habitat.

[1] 'The Hero': *Epitaphs and Occasions* (Lehmann).

7

W. H. Auden

WHEN WE read through the work of any poet of stature, we are left with the sense of some unifying vision. Subtle it may be and impossible to pin down by critical analysis, but we feel its presence. It is not just a question of atmosphere or an individual tone of voice. If it were only this, Edward Lear and Lewis Carroll would be major poets, for their verse certainly communicates the exact tone and quality of themselves.

There must be this atmosphere—it is a condition of communication between writer and reader—but it is not enough for a poet's work just to taste of himself. In major poetry there is also some central vision which seems to use the poet in order to express itself, and round which the ideas and images of his work are constellated.

This vision is the quick of his poetic life. He does not choose it, it chooses him. Perhaps it is difficult to separate its development from the maturation of his own personality, certainly it cannot be separated from his technique. Only in minor work is one conscious of technical brilliance, the tour-de-force; in great verse one is only aware that its statements are accurate; in other words that they correspond to the poet's vision. When this correspondence takes place, then the poet, his technique and the vision are fused into an organic unity which is the poem. It is as meaningless to question the relevance of this unity to life as any other living phenomenon, a horse, for instance, or grandfather's cough.

In the work of W. H. Auden (b. 1907) it is extremely difficult to find such a central vision. Richard Hoggart attempts to sum up the intentions of his poetry: 'Auden combines an intense interest in the human heart with a desire to reform society and he thinks our psychological ills greater than our political. . . . He is convinced of the urgent need for mental therapy; he believes that the spread and assimilation of the findings of psychology can help society towards health; he is sure that such action is morally desirable; he thinks it is owed to "the human creature we must nurse to sense and decency".'[1]

Now it is perfectly true that such good intentions as these are present in Auden's poetry. But like other critiques of what Auden's work is about, Hoggart's remarks seem to slide away from the reality of his verse. It is certainly true that he makes many observations about man and society and that these observations have about them a certain continuity. But it is difficult to take them seriously. We may not be able to share the life and knowledge of Dante, Baudelaire or Blake, but we know that these men mean what they say. They are behind the truths of their poetry because they paid for them with their life. Unlike minor verse, their poetry is not just a question of atmosphere, felicities and word music, but of certain conceptions of life and death which are held with absolute seriousness.

Robert Graves dismisses Auden by saying that his real talent is for light verse, and in Auden's 'Letter to Lord Byron' the poet has suggested just this about his own work:

> You must ask me who
> Have written just as I'd have liked to do.
> I stop to listen and the names I hear
> Are those of Firbank, Potter, Carroll, Lear.

In the face of such disarming modesty it seems unfair to criticise Auden for lacking the 'high seriousness' which Matthew Arnold sought for in poetry. But whatever his fantasies may be it is simply not true that his work and talent bear much relationship to the writers he mentions. It is true that he has the playful touch and an ability to create a mirror world of nostalgia:

> —'O for doors to be open and an invite with gilded edges
> To dine with Lord Lobcock and Count Asthma on the platinum
> benches,
> With somersaults and fireworks, the roast and the smacking
> kisses'—
> Cried the cripples to the silent statue,
> The six beggared cripples.

[1] RICHARD HOGGART: *Auden* (Chatto and Windus, 1951).

But Auden's talents are very considerable and, unlike Edward Lear, Firbank and so on, he is concerned with ideas. The trouble is that he seems to disappear from behind them like the Cheshire Cat from its grin. With Yeats or Eliot one feels that their ideas grew out of their own personal commitment, and then were supported by their reading. They seem to have been selected by their themes. But Auden appears to choose his themes. Marx, Freud, Kierkegaard; one suspects, at times, that he takes the conceptions of those writers who are current and fashionable, for his talent to versify:

> A pantheist not a solipsist, he cooperates
> With a universe of large and noisy feeling-states
> Without troubling to place
> Them anywhere special, for, to his eyes, Funnyface
> Or Elephant as yet
> Mean nothing. His distinction between Me and Us
> Is a matter of taste; his seasons are Dry and Wet;
> He thinks as his mouth does.[1]

The content of this passage about a newborn baby is grist for Auden's skill. It is difficult to think that it is part of his own living process or would matter more to him than a dozen other similar ideas. He has chosen an idea from a book and turned it into a 'copy of verses'.

Eliot writes of Tennyson and Browning that they 'are poets and they think; but they do not feel their thought as immediately as the odour of a rose. A thought to Donne was an experience; it modified his sensibility.'[2] In Auden there is perhaps a deeper split between the thinker and the poet than in Browning or Tennyson. It is not merely that he does not feel his thought, but that when he seeks to apprehend a thought poetically and transmute it into the medium of his verse he tends to belittle it. For instance in 'New Year Letter' he illustrates the conception that human life is a process of becoming, not a state of completed being. Isolated moments of completed being may occur during

[1] 'Mundus et Infans.'
[2] T. S. ELIOT: 'The Metaphysical Poets.' From *Selected Essays*.

the process, but we cannot hold to ourselves these moments of illumination. Blake wrote about this duality with accuracy; presumably because to him it was a lived experience:

> He who bends to himself a Joy
> Doth the wingéd life destroy;
> But he who kisses the Joy as it flies
> Lives in Eternity's sunrise.[1]

But, as John Bayley has pointed out in *The Romantic Survival*, when Auden deals with this concept he uses an image which is amusing, but ghost-story stuff, pure M. R. James:

> The sky grows crimson with a curse,
> The flowers change colour for the worse,
> He hears behind his back the wicket
> Padlock itself, from the dark thicket
> The chuckle with no healthy cause,
> And, helpless, sees the crooked claws
> Emerging into view and groping
> For handholds on the low round coping,
> As horror clambers from the well:
> For he has sprung the trap of hell.[2]

Now this is very sensible verse, and provided one forgets what it is about there is complete assent. But the fact remains that it is supposed to express the desperate state of mind which ensues when we try to nail down our process of becoming to a single moment of time. Auden not only fails to do justice to this theme, his verse reduces it to clever whimsy. What a poet should do is communicate in one statement both the idea and the growing pains which lie behind it. What Auden does, all too often, is skilfully translate the idea into cosy *Boys' Own Paper* images which bear little or no relationship to life. It is as if he gave us the impression that he had tamed some fierce stallion just by a lump of sugar and his skilful equestrian hand. For a few seconds,

[1] 'Gnomic Verses.'
[2] 'New Year Letter.'

'Marvellous,' we murmur, 'this indeed is resolution', but then we look a little closer and realise that all he has actually mastered is the old towel horse and a fur rug. Auden is a great tamer:

> He from these lands of terrifying mottoes
> Makes worlds as innocent as Beatrix Potter's;

Much that is charmed by the extraordinary technical magic of his more recent poems tends to become a little cosy; even death itself:

> The moon is up there, but without warning,
> A little before dawn,
> Miss Lovely, life and soul of the party,
> Wakes with a dreadful start,
> Sure that whatever—O God! she is in for
> Is about to begin,
> Or hearing, beyond the hushabye noises
> Of sea and Me, just a voice
> Ask as one might the time or a trifle
> Extra her money and her life.

That is the conclusion of 'Pleasure Island', a poem which deals among other things with the intrusion of Eternity into time and the traffic of flesh. But, somehow, Auden the magician draws out the sting which should lie in the tail of his great subject. The woman is removed from her humanity by the abstraction 'Miss Lovely' and the cliché, 'life and soul of the party'. We are buffered from her agony by the knowledge that she 'wakes with a *dreadful* start'. After all this happens when the alarm clock goes off too early, or the cat is sick in the passage. 'O God,' on the face of it seems exact enough, but it is so placed in the line that it evokes 'My dear,' the exaggerated gasp of cocktail gossip. The impersonal *Sea* and the personal *Me* are linked together, since both make 'hushabye noises', and death is gentled down to a highwayman, demanding in the traditional language of such gentlemen of the road, 'her money and her life'.

This is cogent witty verse and highly skilful. I suspect that very cerebral people are partial to Auden's poetry, since it justifies the intellectual's tendency to split heart and head, shadow and substance, wisdom and knowledge. No doubt they would say that through his Miss Lovely, 'Life and soul of the party', and so on, he is translating a traditional theme into terms which are personal and contemporary. But the point is that he is writing about death; a passage like this placed besides Eliot's treatment of a similar theme in the conclusion to 'Gerontion', withers like candy floss near a bonfire:

> What will the spider do,
> Suspend its operations, will the weevil
> Delay? De Bailhache, Fresca, Mrs. Cammel, whirled
> Beyond the circuit of the shuddering Bear
> In fractured atoms. Gull against the wind, in the windy straits
> Of Belle Isle, or running on the Horn,
> White feathers in the snow, the Gulf claims,
> And an old man driven by the Trades
> To a sleepy corner.

But Auden has authentic gifts and these draw him to the traditional themes, and at times to make the affirmation of great poetry. This ending to his elegy 'In Memory of Sigmund Freud' for example:

> One rational voice is dumb; over a grave
> The household of Impulse mourns one dearly loved.
> Sad is Eros, builder of cities,
> And weeping anarchic Aphrodite.

In passages like this, and there are many of them, indeed many whole poems of such quality, it is almost as if the poet who could have used more constantly such major gifts, had broken through the personality of Auden and spoken for himself. Too often the voice of the poet is drowned by the chatter of the don, teacher and uncle, who are also constituents of this human being.

Not that the statements of the don are without point. This passage from 'Alonzo to Ferdinand', from 'The Mirror and the

Sea' is excellent didactic verse, in the vein of Kipling's 'If' and with the same degree of good sense and sureness, but with much greater visual impact:

> But should you fail to keep your kingdom
> And, like you father before you, come
> Where thought accuses and feeling mocks,
> Believe your pain; praise the scorching rocks
> For their dessication of your lust,
> Thank the bitter treatment of the tide
> For its dissolution of your pride,
> That the whirlpool may arrange your will
> And the deluge release it to find
> The spring in the desert, the fruitful
> Island in the sea, where flesh and mind
> Are delivered from mistrust.

This is of the same sound, workaday stuff as:

> If you can fill the unforgiving minute
> With sixty seconds worth of distance run
> Yours is the earth and all that there is in it
> And what is more you'll be a man, my son.

No doubt as the clock moves on, young poets will write about 'horrible old Auden' as he wrote about 'horrible old Kipling', but that will not alter the sterling worth of his advice or the craftsmanship of his verse. The trouble is, though, that Auden the man is at times stronger than Auden the poet. There is something cross-grained in the man, and so he often uses his poetic gift to make everything a trifle smaller than actual life. Auden attempts to whittle down the phenomena of life, rather than serve the poetic task and show how these phenomena shade off into a mystery which exceeds them, and of which they are the inadequate metaphors.

At first sight one imagines he is using his verse to make the world accessible to our limited awareness, helping us to assimilate both ourselves and the difficult creatures which surround us. But often it is more a question of making small and common-place than of assimilation. When touched by the magic wand of his poetry, human beings and things do become accessible to our limited human consciousness, but very often they also cease to be what they are. Lakes, for instance, dwindle from whatever reality Wordsworth saw in them to an urbane and urban joke. Humorous, but such a tiny snippet from our deeper apprehension, that we feel a trifle embarrassed at enjoying it.

> A lake allows an average father, walking slowly,
> To circumvent it in an afternoon,
> And any healthy mother to halloo the children
> Back to her bedtime from their games across:
> (Anything bigger than that, like Michigan or Baikal,
> Though potable, is an 'estranging sea'.)

> .   .   .   .   .

> It is unlikely I shall ever keep a swan
> Or build a tower on any small trombolo,
> But that's not going to stop me wondering what sort
> Of lake I should decide on if I should.
> Moraine, pot, oxbow, glint, sink, crater, piedmont, dimple... ?
> Just reeling off their names is ever so comfy.[1]

Auden's is a tripper's vision of nature and 'comfy' is the word which best describes it. At his best, in 'Plains', his comments are like that of a very good guide book, and give us a great deal of extremely lively and palatable information:

> It's horrible to think what peaks come down to,
> That pecking rain and squelching glacier defeat
> Tall pomps of stone where goddesses lay sleeping,
> Dreaming of being woken by some chisel's kiss,
> That what those blind brutes leave when they are through is
>   nothing,
> But a mere substance, a clay that meekly takes
> The potter's cuff, a gravel that as concrete
> Will unsex any space that it encloses.[2]

[1] 'Lakes.' From *Bucolics*.
[2] 'Plains.' From *Bucolics*.

Verse like this gives us outside information about the forces of erosion, but no inside, that is to say poetical, knowledge of a real mountain or a plain. It is not in the least relevant to 'tall pomps of stone' to say they are dreaming of being woken by some 'chisel's kiss'! That is a literary conceit, and has no relationship to the crags which Auden has hung it on.

Poetical knowledge implies a surrender of the knower to what he knows. Wordsworth could write accurately about mountains because he had been part of an experience which included him and them. It is not just a question of observation, however accurate, but of participation.

> Oh! when I have hung
> Above the raven's nest, by knots of grass
> And half-inch fissures in the slippery rock
> But ill-sustained, and almost (so it seemed)
> Suspended by the blast that blew amain,
> Shouldering the naked crag, oh, at that time
> While on the perilous ridge I hung alone,
> With what strange utterance did the loud dry wind
> Blow through my ear! the sky seemed not a sky
> Of earth—and with what motion moved the clouds![1]

It is the completeness of his opening to what is, the fact of the crag and the sky, which enables Wordsworth to understand what lies behind them, the 'something far more deeply interfused'. Because he has known in this way, it does not seem didacticism when he follows up the physical experience of climbing with the utterance,

> Dust as we are, the immortal spirit grows
> Like harmony in music; there is a dark
> Inscrutable workmanship that reconciles
> Discordant elements, makes them cling together
> In one society. . . .

The second and general observation leads logically from the first, and they are inseparable.

[1] *The Prelude*, Book I.

When Auden writes about mountains he seems to regard them, guide book in one hand and telescope in the other, from some village in the valley. There is no openness to these presences of rock and ice and snow, but a coy suspicion. There must be something wrong with people like mountaineers who are devoted to such inhospitable places.

> And it is curious how often in steep places
> You meet someone short who frowns,
> A type you catch beheading daisies with a stick:
> Small crooks flourish in big towns,
> But perfect monsters—remember Dracula—
> Are bred on crags in castles; those unsmiling parties,
> Clumping off at dawn in the gear of their mystery
> For points up, are a bit alarming;
> They have the balance, nerve,
> And habit of the Spiritual, but what God
> Does their Order serve?[1]

Such verse is so pleasant and well tailored that one is almost willing to forgive the fact that its rhetorical question is completely meaningless, since mountaineers are not serving any god at all, only mountains.

> To be sitting in privacy, like a cat
> On the warm roof of a loft,
> Where the high-spirited son of some gloomy tarn
> Comes sprinting down through a green croft,
> Bright with flowers laid out in exquisite splodges,
> Like a Chinese poem, while, near enough, a real darling
> Is cooking a delicious lunch, would keep me happy for
> What? Five minutes? For an uncatlike
> Creature who has gone wrong,
> Five minutes on even the nicest mountain
> Is awfully long.[2]

[1] From 'Mountains': *Bucolics*.
[2] *Ibid.*

In lines like this it is as if Auden has chosen to look down the wrong end of a telescope, so that mountain, tarn and stream shed their size and quality and become very small indeed, the cheerful setting of a children's story. It tells you very little about mountains, but it does say something about Auden himself. I suspect that what has made him reduce his mountains and lakes to such nursery garden proportions is dread. Dread is partly the realisation that the Ego, myself, as a physical presence in a single moment of time, has about as much chance of encompassing the timeless reaches of the human being as a pint pot has of containing the sea. Now we are often shocked into this realisation by the inhuman otherness of the living and dead creatures which surround us. Mountains, lakes, rivers, plains and the night— Wordsworth realised that these have not only a life of their own, but because of their alien majesty and a kind of familiar remoteness, can make us aware of heights and depths within ourselves which are more than what is usually considered human.

> When into air had partially dissolved
> That vision, given to spirits of the night
> And three chance human wanderers, in
> Calm thought
> Reflected, it appeared to me the type
> Of a majestic intellect, its acts
> And its possessions, what it has and craves,
> What in itself it is, and would become.
> There I beheld the emblem of a mind
> That feeds upon infinity, that broods
> Over the dark abyss, intent to hear
> Its voices issuing forth to silent light
> In one continuous stream. . . .[1]

It is possible that Auden has a deep-seated fear of the mystery and boundlessness both of man himself and nature. This may be why he reduces a mountain stream to the 'high spirited son of some gloomy mountain tarn', and makes it 'spring through a green croft bright with flowers laid out in exquisite splodges'; a

[1] From the Conclusion to *The Prelude*: the ascent of Snowdon.

pleasing picture, but considerably less related to actuality than the water colours of Beatrix Potter. Everything, including the poet himself, must be reduced to a playtime world which is smaller than life. It is not just a tasteful unwillingness to assume the bardic robe and strut which makes Auden refer to himself as 'an uncatlike creature who has gone wrong'. It is an attempt to avoid the painful truth of personality and its growing pains.

His talent conducts him to the border of this understanding; in the poem about Plains, for instance,

> On them, in brilliant moonlight, I have lost my way
> And stood without a shadow at the dead centre
> Of an abominable desolation,
> Like Tarquin ravished by his post-coital sadness.

Here we are convinced that the feeling is genuine, but he follows such admirable verse by a conclusion which neatly gelds it. It was only a game after all.

> Which goes to show I've reason to be frightened
> Not of plains, of course, but of me. I should like
> —Who wouldn't?—to shoot beautifully and be obeyed,
> (I should like also to own a cave with two exits);
> I wish I weren't so silly. . . .

There is some odd lack of participation here between Auden and his own poetry. I do not think it is being humourless and solemn to say there is a rift between the poet 'like Tarquin ravished by his post-coital sadness', and the middle aged adolescent who would like to own a cave with two exits and wishes he weren't so silly.

It almost seems that Auden, the man, has never grown up to Auden the poet. So often just where the man's intelligence should implement and fortify the poet's intuition, it only belittles the verse and takes it from its true direction. 'The Willow Wren and the Stare' is a poem about lovers overlooked by two birds. Its tenderness and wisdom would be satisfactorily fulfilled by the rhythms and refrain if it were not for the occasional

intrusion into the syntax of something which seems unfortunately
alien to the poem's intention.

> Waking in her arms, he cried,
> Utterly content;
> 'I have heard the high good noises,
> Promoted for an instant,
> Stood upon the shining outskirts
> Of that Joy I thank
> For you, my dog and every goody!'
> There on the grass bank
> She laughed, he laughed, they laughed together,
> Then they ate and drank:
> *Did he know what he meant?* said the willow-wren—
> *God only knows*, said the stare.

But how one may well ask, how by all that is holy, have 'my dog
and every goody' crept into the picture. And from Auden himself one suspects, some undigested impulse, the poet would never
strike such a false note.

Auden has made some general declamation about the nature
and status of poetry in both his verse and his prose,

> For poetry makes nothing happen: it survives
> In the valley of its choice where executives
> Would never want to tamper. . . .[1]

It is a kind of game played by children and opposed to the
serious business of living with which grown-ups are busy. It
is not a question of poetry making judgments about a serious
situation but of creating a world which is autonomous and a
fiction. 'All the phenomena of an empirically ordinary world
are given. Extended objects appear to which events happen—
old men catch dreadful coughs, little girls get their arms twisted,
flames run whooping through woods, round a river bend,
as harmless looking as a dirty old bearskin rug, comes the
gliding fury of a town-effacing wave, but these are merely

[1] 'In Memory of W. B. Yeats.'

G

elements in an allegorical landscape to which mathematical measurement and phenomenological analysis have no relevance.'[1] Unless one is prepared to believe that the entire area of subjective experience with which poetry is concerned is unreal, and its exploration by great poets, mystics and psychologists quite meaningless, such argument is false nonsense. Perhaps it proceeds from some difficulty Auden may have in entering the arena of his poetry. It is always extremely hard for any poet to implement even a few of the aspirations of his verse within his personal life. In Auden this schism between personality and work is, perhaps, unusually great; it is difficult to understand otherwise his tendency to belittle the function of poetry, indeed of all the arts.

> Shame at our shortcomings make
> Lame magicians of us all,
> Forcing our inventions to
> An illegal miracle
> And a theatre of disguise. . . .[2]

He has justified his personal predicament by the Freudian theory that the artist retreats from a harsh reality to a world of fantasy:

> Here on dark nights where worlds of triumph sleep
> Lost love in abstract speculation burns,
> And exiled Will to politics returns
> In epic verse that lets its traitors weep.[3]

But the point is the accuracy of the return: the artist only deserves his name if he wrestles from the unconscious certain truths which have relevance to a man and his life. Somehow Auden has managed to by-pass this extreme relevance. Such a schism between heart and head, imagination and reality, may be sympathetic to a certain public, but this does not alter the fact that Auden has often subordinated a major poetical gift to a minor and very private statement.

[1] 'Caliban to the Audience': Chapter III of 'The Sea and the Mirror.' *For the Time Being.'*
[2] 'Epithalamium.'
[3] No. IX. 'The Quest'—*New Year Letter.*

8

Stephen Spender — Cecil Day Lewis — Louis MacNeice

IT IS often said that the poetry of Stephen Spender (b. 1909) is about pity, the pathos and weakness of man, and more particularly of the poet's own shortcomings.

In the preface to his own poems Wilfred Owen said: 'My subject is War and the pity of War. The Poetry is in the pity. Yet these elegies are to this generation in no sense consolatory. They may be to the next. All a poet can do today is warn. That is why the true Poets must be truthful.' And Owen's poetry is truthful. War shocked him into a vision of the tragedy of mankind which is both profound and mature, and his verse served this vision faithfully.

> Move him into the sun—
> Gently its touch awoke him once,
> At home, whispering of fields unsown.
> Always it woke him, even in France,
> Until this morning and this snow.
> If anything might rouse him now
> The kind old sun will know.

> Think how it wakes the seeds,
> Woke, once, the clays of a cold star.
> Are limbs, so dear-achieved, are sides,
> Full—nerved—still warm—too hard to stir?
> Was it for this the clay grew tall?
> —O what made fatuous sunbeams toil
> To break earth's sleep at all?[1]

[1] 'Futility.' The Poems of Wilfred Owen (Chatto).

It is interesting to set this poem of Owen's beside the beginning and ending of Spender's 'Ultima Ratio Regum', since both poems have the same theme, a man killed by war.

> The guns spell money's ultimate reason
> In letters of lead on the spring hillside.
> But the boy lying dead under the olive trees
> Was too young and too silly
> To have been notable to their important eye.
> He was a better target for a kiss.
>
> .   .   .   .   .
>
> Consider his life which was valueless
> In terms of employment, hotel ledgers, news files.
> Consider. One bullet in ten thousand kills a man.
> Ask. Was so much expenditure justified
> On the death of one so young and so silly
> Lying under the olive trees, O world, O death?

There is a tremendous urgency about Owen's poem. Its opening lines confront us directly with the dead soldier because the poet has seen and been involved in his death. The soldier is the poem, not what the poem is about. Because Owen has shared in the experience of this death his verse is able to express the double reality of the soldier. He is one human being and dead, but he also suggests the whole tragedy of mankind.

Spender seems to have used the dead soldier of the Spanish War as a subject to write a poem about. He is not implicated in his disaster. If he were he could never have written, 'He was a better target for a kiss', a remark which is quite inappropriate. It is not a question of immediacy, 'of *this* morning and *this* snow', for the shock of the event is softened, almost glamourised by its decorative background of spring hillside and olive trees. Finally the fact of death is neatly sidestepped by the euphemism, 'so young and so silly'.

Spender can turn verses with skill and elegance, and when his work is concerned with themes which really do impinge on his personal life, such as jealousy or infidelity, then it can show deep understanding and pathos.

However, when he is concerned with subjects which although tragic and violent have a more general significance, one has at times the feeling that he is treating of them because they are the sort of thing a poet ought to write about. When Spender's deeper sympathies are not involved with his theme, then he tends to use it as a nucleus, a nucleus round which his sensitivity and delight in the colour of words can wear a dazzling mesh, which one might be tempted to call a kind of literary candy floss. It is difficult for instance to realise that these lines have anything to do with a Spanish poet being blown to pieces by a bomb, yet this is the ostensible subject of their poem:

> Then, stupidly, the sulphur stucco pigeon
>   Fixed to the gable above your ceiling
>   Swooped in a curve before your window
>   Uttering, as it seemed, a coo.
>   When you smiled.
> Everything in the room was shattered,
>   Only you remained whole
>   In frozen wonder, as though you stared
>   At your image in the broken mirror
>   Where it had always been silverly carried.[1]

Every now and again a poem of Spenders stands out from the company it's in, 'Ice', for example, or the Song which begins, 'Stranger, you who hide my love'. Such poems have been deeply felt and the feeling has gone into the language and made it alive. At the opposite extreme some of his poems have a repetitive sameness. When pigs entered the factory of Upton Sinclair they came out as sausages; when real life enters Stephen Spender's poetic machinery it sometimes comes out as a euphemism. This would not matter, perhaps, if the poet was treating of bluebell woods, but when it's a question of war guilt as in 'Responsibility: the Pilots who destroyed Germany, Spring 1945,' then the effect can be embarrassing.

[1] 'To a Spanish Poet.'

I stood on a roof-top and they wove their cage,
Their murmuring, throbbing cage, in the air of blue crystal
I saw them gleam above the town like diamond bolts
Conjoining invisible struts of wire,
Carrying through the sky their squadron's cage
Woven by instincts delicate as a shoal of flying fish. . . .

Now I tie the ribbons torn down from those terraces
Around the hidden image in my lines,
And my life which never paid the price of their wounds,
Turns thoughts over and over like a propeller,
Assumes their guilts, honours, repents, prays for them.

Images should serve the poem as a whole, be subordinate to its theme, but in verse like this they have taken complete control of the poem so that its verdict and intention are lost under them, like a wooden trellis under a riot of roses.

Spender writes, 'And my life which never paid the price of their wounds.' One feels some of his verse has not paid the price of its subject. Even in 'Memento', a poem about the German concentration camps, the edge of the terrible subject is blunted by images—bird-song-fretted air, dove, begging bowls—which are too 'poetic' to serve it truthfully.

Remember the blackness of that flesh
Tarring the bones with a thin varnish
Belsen Theresenstadt Buchenwald where
Faces were clenched despair
Knocking at the bird-song-fretted air.

Their eyes sunk jellied in their holes
Were held towards the sun like begging bowls
Their hands like rakes with fingernails of rust
Scratched for a little kindness from the dust.
To many, in its beak, no dove brought answer.[1]

[1] 'Memento': *Collected Poems.*

In an earlier poem Spender wrote about the Unemployed,

> No I will weave no tracery of pen ornament
> To make them birds upon my singing tree . . . .

But in some of his poems it is exactly this that seems to be happening. One is grateful to him when his work illuminates the personal situations of loneliness and humiliation which we are all involved in. But it is not possible to give beauty treatment to Belsen or a dead soldier. After 'Memento' one turns with a certain relief to a poem by D. J. Enright on a similar theme. It is called 'No Offence, Berlin'; there is little beauty in it or flowering speech but it does seem accurate.

> In no country
> Are the disposal services more efficient.
>
> Standardised dustbins
> Fit precisely into the mouth of a large cylinder
> Slung on a six-wheeled chassis.
> Even the dustbin lid is raised mechanically
> At the very last moment.
> You could dispose of a corpse like this
> Without giving the least offence.
>
> In no country
> Are the public lavatories more immaculately kept.
> As neat as new pins, smelling of pine forests,
> With a roar like distant Wagner
> Your sins are washed away.
>
> In no country
> Do the ambulances arrive more promptly.
> You are lying on the stretcher
> Before the police, the driver, the byestanders and the
>   neighbouring shopkeepers
> Have finished lecturing you.

In no country
Are the burial facilities more foolproof.
A few pfennigs a week, according to age,
Will procure you a very decent funeral.
You merely sign on the dotted line
And keep your payments regular.

In no country
Are the disposal services more efficient
—I reflect—
As I am sorted out, dressed down, lined up,
Shepherded through the door
Marshalled across the smooth-faced asphalt,
And fed into the mouth of a large cylinder
Labelled 'Lufthansa'.[1]

Although he has an unfortunate tendency to write really appalling, keepsake verses for public occasions such as Royal Birthdays—this seems a kind of nervous tick—Cecil Day Lewis (b. 1904) is usually an honest poet. He does not versify ideas or luxuriate in images for their own sake, since his gift seems dovetailed to his personal experience and he uses it to serve certain conceptions which are his poetic life.

To understand this truthfulness of Day Lewis one must take his work as a whole. The principal theme which runs through it is that of duality, the opposition between life and death, with which every human being is concerned.

There is a dark room,
The locked and shuttered tomb,
Where negative's made positive.
Another dark room,
The blind and bolted tomb,
Where positives change to negative.

[1] D. J. ENRIGHT: 'No Offence: Berlin.' From *Some Men are Brothers* (Chatto and Windus). See page 151.

We may not undo
That or escape this, who
Have birth and death coiled in our bones.
Nothing we can do
Will sweeten the real rue,
That we begin, and end, with groans.

These two short verses from an early volume, *From Feathers to Iron* state baldly the theme which much of his work elaborates. We contain within ourselves both life and death, and the fact that we are living means that we are also dying. Yeats, Eliot, and Muir also have this deep realisation of human impermanence, but their response to it is a religious one. For these poets, man is not summed up by time and place, and the body is but one mode of expression for a spiritual process of which death itself is only an incident. We must rejoice in time and decay because we are not limited by time or our perishing bodies:

An aged man is but a paltry thing
A tattered coat upon a stick, unless
Soul clap its hands and sing, and louder sing
For every tatter in its mortal dress. . . .[1]

Day Lewis's response to mutability is not religious. Like some Elizabethan poets he feels that the shadow of death gives an extreme zest and meaning to the present moment:

I sang as one
Who on a tilting deck sings
To keep men's courage up, though the wave hangs
That shall cut off their sun.

As storm-cocks sing,
Flinging their natural answer to the winds' teeth,
And care not if it is waste of breath
Or birth carol of spring.

[1] W. B. YEATS: 'Sailing to Byzantium'.

This is a tragic attitude. It is not a question of nostalgia for the past, or of longing for the future, but of the fulness of our response to the present moment which is doomed but quick with life:

> The red advance of life
> Contracts pride, calls out the common blood,
> Beats song into a single blade,
> Makes a depth charge of grief.
>
> Move then with new desires,
> For where we used to build and love
> Is no mans land, and only ghosts can live
> Between two fires. . . .[1]

It is true that in the first poem of *From Feathers to Iron* he suggests that later on he may have something to say about an existence beyond time:

> Some say we walk out of time altogether
> This way into a region where the primrose
> Shows an immortal dew, sun at meridian
> Stands up forever and in scent the lime tree.
> *This is a land which later we may tell of. . . .*

But he has not told us about it yet. What he has done is to deepen and elaborate his awareness of the tension between life and death.

His delight in all the varieties of life would be almost that of the virtuoso reporter skimming over the surface, if it were not counterbalanced by his realisation of how transitory it is:

> 'Therefore I'd browse on the skin of things, the delicate field of Diversity, skimming gold from the buttercup, dust from the nettle.'

[1] 'The Conflict.'

says one of the characters of 'An Italian Visit'. But Day Lewis himself is aware that death lies under the skin of things, and this belief gives pathos to his verse:

> It is love's way
> To shine most through the slow dusk of adieu.
> Long may it glow within us, that timeless halycon halt
> On our rough journey back to clay.
> Oh, may my farewell word, may this your elegy
> Written in life blood from a condemned heart
> Be quick and haunting even beyond our day.[1]

I believe that the vision of Yeats or Eliot of the human being is probably more exact, and that it is impossible to identify ourselves completely with any one aspect of our temporal life, since we are a spiritual process. But the fact remains that to see a man in this way tends to dehumanise him. 'Gerontion', 'Crazy Jane', 'Cuchualain' have become what perhaps we really are, beneath the masks of outward appearance, energy itself, thought, conflict. But in achieving this timeless significance they have shed much of their ordinary humanity. That may be commonplace and transitory but it is what evokes compassion. Like Thomas Hardy, with whom he has great sympathy, Day Lewis usually sees the human being as synonymous with his tragic situation in the present moment. Such a vision may be only half the truth, but it does hold the person before us, evoke our tenderness. Here is part of his poem about a girl nursing her doll in a shelter during an air raid. She is described precisely, and for Day Lewis her maternal solicitude is an assertion of life and the answer to death's negation:

> Genius could never paint the maternal pose
> More deftly than accident had roughed it there,
> Setting amidst our terrors against the glare
> Of unshaded bulb and whitewashed brick, that rose.

[1] 'Elegy before Death: At Settignano.'

Instinct was hers and an earthquake hour revealed it
In flesh—the meek-laid lashes, the glint in the eye
Defying wrath and reason, the arms that shielded
A plaster doll from an erupting sky.

No argument for living could long sustain
These ills: it needs a faithful eye, to have seen all
Love in the drop of a lash and tell it eternal
By one pure bead of its dew-dissolving chain.

Dear sheltering child, if again misgivings grieve me
That love is only a respite, an opal bloom
Upon our snow-set fields, come back to revive me
Cradling your spark through blizzard, drift and tomb.[1]

Like that of Day Lewis, the poetry of Louis MacNeice (b. 1907) derives its force from a realisation of the impermanence and yet intense significance of human life. He is not involved with Yeats's imperishable 'Byzantium' or T. S. Eliot's 'still point beyond the turning world', but with the ebb and flow of all the creatures of life between their polarities of birth and dying.

So, of course, are Yeats and Eliot, but with these poets there is always the struggle to apprehend some single state of being beyond the flux, a wholeness which resolves the duality of decaying flesh and imperishable spirit. For MacNeice the raw flux of existence is enough.

This does not mean, as has sometimes been suggested, that he is a shallow writer, a mere poetic journalist. 'Journalist' gives the impression of someone who whisks up superficial information about events and people with whom he is not in the least involved. But MacNeice is always implicated in whatever he writes about. He is not the detached reporter commenting from a safe distance upon 'the busy scene', but a poet who writes with open heart and mind, not about the 'intersection of time with the timeless' but his own humanity as it opens to that of other men and women, and all the varieties of nature:

[1] From 'In the Shelter'.

Lavender blue for love, lavender green for youth—
Never is time to retire.
Let me buy one more bunch and hold myself straight as I can
Not out of pride but out of respect for the truth,
For the gorgeous, though borrowed, fire
Which shone on my cradle and warmed my heart as a man.[1]

Perhaps MacNeice is best in the long autobiographical poem, such as his *Autumn Journal* and *Autumn Sequel*. In these he blends vivid description of London, its suburbs, or Wales, anecdotes about his friends, comments on politics and probings into human nature and destiny. The result is a monologue which is both personal and impersonal. It is always MacNeice talking, yet he goes out to his subject with such imaginative zest that he seems to merge with it, and we get the impression not so much of one man talking as of a whole aspect of contemporary life having become articulate.

He prefaces his *Autumn Sequel* with a statement of Walt Whitman,

> Do I contradict myself?
> Very well then I contradict myself.

For MacNeice's poetry is a kind of celebration. What matters for him is not the logic of the intellect but to capture in verse something of the flavour and fire of living. Ideas have no absolute value for him, they are not essences to be sweated painfully out of the flux, but simply one of its aspects. Nevertheless his poetry does have its distinctive vision. Two of his finest poems contain Autumn in their title, because that season most poignantly evokes evanescence:

> Live as you can
> On land, your body is water, the earth you tread
> Condemned to end in the puddle where it began.

But for MacNeice as for Day Lewis the point is the assertion of life in the teeth of dissolution, and this assertion colours all his poetry:

[1] 'Notes for a Biography': *London Magazine*, April 1959.

We have not locked the door, having lost both script and staff
We have kept our pilgrims' legs; though the meaning fails
We still can double the surviving half
And put some flesh upon it. This is Wales,
A matter of flesh and rock. This is a room
Of living people. Nothing perhaps avails
Against the sea like rock, like doomed men against doom.[1]

[1] *Autumn Sequel.*

9

Dylan Thomas

If one has the stomach to add the breakages, upheavals, inversions of all this chambermade music one stands, given a grain of good-will, a fair chance of actually seeing the whirling dervish, Tumult, son of Thunder, self exiled in upon his ego, a nightlong a shaking betwixtween white or red hawrors, noonday terrorised to skin and bone by an ineluctable phantom (may the Shaper have mercy on him!) writing the mystery of himself in furniture.

JAMES JOYCE: *Finnegans Wake*, page 184.

LITERARY CRITICISM has certainly made a long journey from the rumbustious days of the Edinburgh Review. Robert Graves, it is true, still lays about him with the same old blackthorn cudgel wielded by Jeffries. But as a whole such instruments have been superseded by the surgeon's scalpel and microscope. It is no longer a question of thundering 'X is a bad poet, I know for a fact he drinks, sleeps with his parlour maid and has a Tyneside accent', but of carefully pointing out just why his adjectives are tired and shopsoiled, his rhythms inappropriate to his subject matter and his images trite. It is even suggested that literary criticism has become a science.

What that presumably amounts to is that its practitioners have taken an English Degree and have some knowledge of the theory and practice of Dr. I. A. Richards, and Dr. F. R. Leavis. The trouble is that poems are not pieces of fibre or protoplasm which can be adequately known by certain techniques of measurement and chemical analysis. Provided a scientist has a high I.Q. and a gift for figures, he can do justice to a molecule even if emotionally he has stayed all of a piece at the age of fourteen. A molecule is not, as a rule, an emotional experience; a poem is. Consequently, though a literary critic may have accumulated every letter in the academic alphabet, as far as degrees go, and have enough information about prosody and syntax to fill an encyclopoedia, it will profit him absolutely nothing in his knowledge of a poem unless his emotional development is such that he can make an adequate response.

The knowledge of a poem is not merely cerebral but of the whole man. Information about prosody and so on is a useful tool, but ultimately poetic knowledge can only be won by the kind of suffering which one can call 'growing pains', and this is not a question of the lecture room and is far rarer than Ph.Ds.

Provided the poetic ground has been well ploughed before and the proper answers furrowed out by time—I mean that the poet has been well and truly dead for fifty years or so—then the trained literary critic can ply his microscope and scalpel with reasonable accuracy. Even if emotionally he is as a molehill to Mount Everest, he can produce some very interesting sidelines on the great dead. In his quatrain, 'The Poet discovers himself to be infested with lice', David Wright has made a comment on this particular industry:

> At least you feed on me while I'm alive,
> Feeble and sidling parasites! instead
> (Like necrophilic bugs that better thrive)
> Of making a fat living from the dead.[1]

The trouble comes when the critic, however well trained, is confronted by the work of a living poet. Here time has ploughed out no guiding furrows; there is only the lonely communion of the individual with the poems. True there are the 'tools of literary criticism', but tools cannot feel and respond; someone has to use the things.

Just how oddly they can be used when time has given them no blue print to work on is shown by the critical response to the work of John Betjeman. Betjeman (b. 1906) is a very good writer of verse; his status in this field may be comparable to Thomas Hood's. Like a good popular novelist, he completely deserves the fame he has got, and his audience will probably be spread over the wide surface of the present, rather than in depth through time. The survival of his verse may depend on its accurately evoking the flavour of an age, the stock attitudes of a middle class, the

[1] DAVID WRIGHT: *Moral Stories* (Verschoyle).

illusions of niceness and sweet nostalgia for a vanished childhood. Betjeman is also, though much less consistently, a minor poet, who can express with considerable poignancy the vulnerability of childhood and the terror of death. He can also paint a landscape in his poems with something of the sweet and close cleaving to nature which we find in Tennyson and other Victorians.

It is not Betjeman who is depressing, but the fact that trained literary critics can mistake this talented versifier, and at times minor poet, for a poet of the status of Hardy. This we are told is comparable to Hardy at his best; it is from a poem called 'In a Bath Teashop'.

> She such a very ordinary little woman
> He such a thumping crook
> But both for a moment little lower than the angels
> In the tea shop's ingle nook.

Betjeman is popular because his verse has charm, and corresponds to certain widely held attitudes of the British Middle Class. Sometimes a good poet manages to build up an acceptable persona, become poetically 'U' before, or at least immediately after, his death. This has happened to Dylan Thomas (1914–1953). His personality, overshadowed as it was by a most genuine poetic gift, was able to project itself through radio, television, the poetry recital, and its correspondence to some Dionysian Archetype, dear to the Anglo-American heart, into 'many homes'. This was a gift to the critics. Without having recognised him themselves, they were presented with a Grade A, almost as good as fifty years dead, but contemporary poet, to work on.

Thomas was one of those tragic artists whose lives are taken over and dominated by their vision. To some extent all poets are used by their vision in this way, but although he was desperately wrestling for it in his last years, Thomas could never obtain the degree of self-consciousness which would have enabled him to separate himself from his great gift, to become its medium and interpreter, instead of its creature. Consequently he was driven to work out in his own behaviour the polarity between death and life, the one and all, which is the substance of his poetry. Like that of Byron, Keats, Rimbaud or Strindberg, Thomas's life, as time rounds it off from us and makes it whole, will increasingly appear as one of his poems, asserting in all its aspects the same themes of death and resurrection.

This unity of Thomas's life and poetry was his personal tragedy; but it may be responsible for the speedy acceptance of his work by the public, for a life can more easily break through the time barrier and reach a wide audience than a work of art. This is not to depreciate the true merit of his poetry, but I would suggest there are two other poets of the same generation, Vernon Watkins (in one or two of his books) and George Barker, whose work has something of Thomas's quality and power. However, their lives have not achieved any tragic notoriety, and so their public acclaim is comparatively small.

What strikes one about some of the poetry of Barker and Watkins, and a great deal of the work of Dylan Thomas, is that it does not lend itself to critical analysis. Because Thomas has become 'a name' and therefore grist for thesis and memoir, he has certainly been subject to this. But the conscientious attempt to wrestle some kind of prose meaning from such poems as, 'Because the pleasure bird whistles after the hot wires,/ Shall the blind horse sing sweeter',/ or, 'If my head hurt a hare's foot,/ Pack back the downed bone'/, produces in at least one reader only acute boredom.

The point is that many of the poems by Dylan Thomas and a few of those by Barker and Watkins are incantations. Now an incantation is a magic spell or charm to summon up the spirits of the dead or unborn. These poets often use words to conjure up ghosts from those deeper levels of ourselves of which we are not fully conscious. Consequently it is, at times, not a question of their language having a specific reference to some situation of the external, or even of the subjective world, but of its ability to bring out of us into the light of day certain benighted energies of thought and feeling.

Just as the ancient spells to raise the dead had to be effective, so this kind of poetry must exactly touch the springs of our feeling. But what matters is the emotion and thought which come out when the spring is touched. Used in this way, words have power, but it is the power to evoke, rather than make a verifiable remark. So the criticism of such verse should be more concerned with 'What I feel when I read these words', than 'What it is that the words are saying'. They solicit not so much the need for analysis and a checking of references, as autobiographical confession.

Here, for instance, are passages from the work of Vernon Watkins, George Barker and Dylan Thomas. Each one has great incantatory power. But it is the power of the charged word to conjure emotion from within us. It is not meant to be a stricture on these poems when I say there is not one of them but would, to some extent, crumble into banality under the critic's surgery.

Watkins's poem is about a feather which is torn from a seabird by a hawk and falls into the sea:

> Sheer from wide air to wilderness
> The victim fell and lay;
> The starlike bone is fathomless,
> Lost among wind and spray.
> This lonely, isolated thing
> Trembles amid their sound.
> I set my finger on the string
> That spins the ages round.
> But let it sleep, let it sleep
> Where shell and stone are cast;
> Its ecstasy the Furies keep,
> For nothing here is past.
> The perfect into night must fly;
> On this the winds agree.
> How could a blind rock satisfy
> The hungers of the sea.[1]

The atmosphere of this poem, the mood which it summons out of us is precise enough. But God preserve it from a thoroughgoing pedagogic onslaught. The last two lines might yield easily enough; one could talk about the opposition between shifting, teeming,

[1] 'The Feather,' *The Ballad of the Mari Lwyd.*

moon-pulled water, and the dead stasis of rock; but the Furies? Just what is the string to which the poet sets his finger? No doubt something could be worked out, but I am doubtful if it would help either the poem or its readers.

The same applies to this passage from Barker's 'News of The World III'. The strength of the poem as a whole is unmistakable, but the heart has reasons not altogether available to the head as to just why a moth 'Died a legend of splendour along the line of my life.' No doubt the head could fetch up a few reasons but they would, I suspect, contribute very little to our appreciation of the poem:

> I garb my wife,
> The wide world of a bride, in devastations.
> She has curled up in my hand, and, like a moth,
> Died a legend of splendour along the line of my life.
> But the congregation of clouds paces in dolour
> Over my head and her never barren belly
> Where we lie, summered, together, a world and I.
> Her birdflecked hair, sunsetting the weather,
> Feathers my eye, she shakes an ear-ring sky,
> And her hand of a country trembles against me.
> The glittering nightriders gambol through
> A zodiac of symbols above our love
> Promising, O my star-crossed, death and disasters.
> But I want breath for nothing but your possession
> Now, now, this summer midnight, before the dawn
> Shakes its bright gun in the sky, before
> The serried battalions of lies and organisations of hate
> Entirely encompass us, buried; before the wolf and friend
> Render us enemies. Before all this,
> Lie one night in my arms and give me peace.[1]

Now from Dylan Thomas, the last two verses of 'I Make this in a Warring Absence':

[1] 'News of the World,' III.

These once-blind eyes have breathed a wind of visions,
The cauldron's root through this once rindless hand
Fumed like a tree, and tossed a burning bird;
With loud, torn tooth and tail and cobweb drum
The crumpled packs fled past this ghost in bloom,
And, mild as pardon from a cloud of pride,
The terrible world my brother bares his skin.

Now in the cloud's big breast lie quiet countries,
Delivered seas my love from her proud place
Walks with no wound, nor lighting in her face,
A calm wind blows that raised the trees like hair
Once where the soft snow's blood was turned to ice.
And though my love pulls the pale, nippled air,
Prides of tomorrow suckling in her eyes,
Yet this I make in a forgiving presence.[1]

It is, of course, quite possible to produce some kind of ramshackle explanation and inadequate prose paraphrase of this passage. In the first verse Dylan Thomas is writing about the coming into time and space of the unborn soul, how it puts on carnality and becomes a human being. Eyes, which were blind before birth, as far as this world goes, now 'breathe a wind of visions', and the 'once rindless hand', that is to say lacking the contour and shape of flesh on bone, now fumes like a tree, and tosses the burning bird of prophecy. Because the poet has been born into his time and circumstance, 'the terrible world, my brother, bares his skin'.

But once we have grasped the general intention of verse like this, it is doubtful whether a detailed analysis of its images is very helpful. If Yeats was using the image of a cauldron or a burning bird, such an analysis would, as F. A. C. Wilson has shown, be well worth while. For Yeats's work is both incantatory and exactly referential to a body of traditional wisdom, where cauldron and bird have a specific meaning. But Dylan Thomas is not using words with Yeats's exactness. If we attempt to pin down his cauldron and burning bird to some exclusive fact, then we may bring the poem to a dead stop. Obviously these words

[1] *Collected Poems of Dylan Thomas.*

affect us because they are charged with associations from the past, perhaps also from the future. But in many of his poems it is the way words contribute to some general climate of emotion and thought which matters. Their term of reference is secondary to their main purpose of summoning out of us those blends of half-conscious emotion and thought which make up this climate.

Poetry like this depends on an uneasy marriage between the poet and that Unconscious, which is the common denominator of himself and other people. Where this union is achieved, where there is a fusion between the poet, the reader, and those levels of being which sustain them both, then Thomas's poetry is deeply moving; a potent spell.

> Shut, too, in a tower of words, I mark
> On the horizon walking like the trees
> The wordy shapes of women, and the rows
> Of the star-gestured children in the park.
> Some let me make you of the vowelled beeches,
> Some of the oaken voices, from the roots
> Of many a thorny shire tell you notes,
> Some let me make you of the water's speeches.

> .   .   .   .   .

> Especially when the October wind
> (Some let me make you of Autumnal spells,
> The spider-tongued, and the loud hill of Wales)
> With fists of turnips punishes the land,
> Some let me make you of the heartless words.
> The heart is drained that, spelling in the scurry
> Of chemic blood, warned of the coming fury.
> By the sea's side hear the dark-vowelled birds.[1]

One can know something about poetry like this. By attaching the attributes of language to the world of nature—vowelled beeches, oaken voices, waters' speeches, 'the spider-tongued and the loud hill of Wales'—Thomas brings himself and his environ-

[1] 'Especially When the October Wind.'

ment into a unity. Like Wordsworth's, much of his poetry is an exploration of himself, and this self expands and becomes almost indistinguishable from its environment. Water, trees and hills all share in the poet's speech and are part of an articulate universe. But it is not rewarding to ask just what the *Some* refers to which Thomas is going to make for us of the vowelled beeches and autumnal spells. Incantatory verse requires our response as a whole; the head alone can tell us little about it.

As I said, poetry like this is uncertain in its effect. Where there is not the exact inner rapport between the poet and the unconscious then his work will tend to break down into mere doodling, a welter of disjointed syntax where words fight haphazardly against each other. This is undoubtedly the case with a number of Thomas's poems, where the effect depends on the occasional lucid phrase breaking out of a bedlam of verbiage. The difficulty is that emotion is always struggling to become knowledge, and consequently verse which, like that of some of Rimbaud and Dylan Thomas, relies mainly upon feeling and intuition, is very hard to sustain. It depends upon a kind of 'participation mystique' with the unconscious, and, since that which is felt is always trying to become that which is known, is probably only tenable for a short while. Certainly in his latest and—I believe—finest work, Thomas seems to have tried to know and make clear what before he had only groped for in darkness, and produced in occasional moments of perception. There is something very moving in his attempt to become more fully aware of his poetic vision. This was the way he was developing; unfortunately he was not able to resolve the far-reaching disturbances of his personality, so the development could not continue.

Dylan Thomas's vision is implicit in most of his work. Here is a particularly clear and direct expression of it from an earlier poem:

> The force that through the green fuse drives the flower
> Drives my green age; that blasts the roots of trees
> Is my destroyer.
> And I am dumb to tell the crooked rose
> My youth is bent by the same wintry fever.

The force that drives the water through the rocks
Drives my red blood; that dries the mouthing streams
Turns mine to wax.
And I am dumb to mouth into my veins
How at the mountain stream the same mouth sucks.

Thomas realised, perhaps as fully, as Wordsworth, Man's at-one-ness with certain non-human energies which are also at work in nature. Now although Wordsworth apprehends this energy from the standpoint of a spectator, and a character as firm as his Westmorland granite, he still dreads the depersonalisation which is a consequence of realising this 'ground' of man and the universe:

'Fallings from us, vanishings;
Blank misgivings of a Creature
Moving about in worlds not realised,
High instincts before which our mortal Nature
Did tremble like a guilty Thing surprised. . . .[1]

And his dread is quite justified. It may be true that ultimately we are these 'instincts' and, in some deep sense, not one but everything. Still, it is true that here in time we are also one, not just infinite process, but a circumscribed human ego. Unless this duality is maintained we lapse completely into the depths of ourselves, and that is disintegration. Far more than Wordsworth, Thomas seems to identify himself with what he calls 'the force that through the green fuse drives the flower'. He is its creature, and consequently the force that drives his green age dominates him and is his destroyer. Perhaps it was partly this identification which led to his alcoholic euphoria and early death; it takes a great deal of self-awareness and poise to put up with being just one finite entity after experiencing all and everything. Certainly Dylan Thomas's celebrations of the universal forces which he most deeply experienced are often followed by a lament for his personal doom:

[1] 'Ode on Intimations of Immortality.'

But dark is a long way.
He, on the earth of the night, alone
With all the living, prays,
Who knows the rocketing wind will blow
The bones out of the hills,
And the scythed boulders bleed, and the last
Rage shattered waters kick
Masts and fishes to the still quick stars,
Faithlessly unto Him

Who is the light of old
And air shaped Heaven where souls grow wild
As horses in the foam:
Oh, let me midlife mourn by the shrined
And druid herons' vows
The voyage to ruin I must run,
Dawn ships clouted aground. . . .[1]

I suggested in an earlier chapter that a condition of knowing
these areas of more than personal thought and feeling and energy
is usually trauma, that it takes some kind of rather disastrous
early experience to shock us out of commonplace awareness into
the further reaches of ourselves. This is the price of an eye which
Odin paid for his gift of prophesy. By experiencing, without
necessarily understanding, their personal confusion, poets like
Rimbaud and Dylan Thomas can achieve an extraordinary
insight into the human condition. But personal confusion
cannot be indefinitely by-passed; in the end it is a question of the
poet's either dying as a man and poet, or facing up to the difficulties which underlie his gift. This is a question of greater awareness, of making lucid and articulate the interwoven but conflicting
forces which determine a human being. I think Yeats, and to
some extent T. S. Eliot, may have undergone the kind of death in
life which this entails. But although, at the end of his life, Dylan
Thomas was acutely aware of the necessity for this change, he
was not able to achieve it.

There is often a desperation about his later verse, as if he knew

[1] 'Poem on his Birthday.

that the self-comprehension which would allow him personal
and artistic development was beyond his reach:

> When I was a half of the man I was
> And serve me right as the preachers warn,
> (Sighed the old ram rod, dying of downfall),
> No flailing calf or cat in a flame
> Or hickory bull in milky grass
> But a black sheep with a crumpled horn,
> At last the soul from its foul mousehole
> Slunk pouting out when the limp time came;
> And I gave my soul a blind, slashed eye,
> Gristle and rind, and a roarer's life,
> And I shoved it into the coal black sky
> To find a woman's soul for a wife.[1]

This is a poem of extreme depression. The limp time has come
and Thomas is no longer able to escape from his personal confusion by the euphoria which he signifies by 'flailing calf or
cat in flame'. His soul is given a blind slashed eye and packed
off skywards, because the poet finds a meeting with this essence
of himself to be unbearable. It is as if he was unable to travel his
depression, to

> Lie down where all the ladders start
> In the foul rag and bone shop of the heart.[2]

What Thomas tried to do was to turn his back on his impasse, and
follow his visionary gift to the furthest limit. That, as we know,
was a hospital in New York where catastrophe finally caught up
with him and finished him off both as a man and as a poet.

Because he tried to escape from himself it does not mean that
Thomas wrote escapist poetry. On the contrary the remarkable
thing about much of the later poetry and his drama, *Under Milk
Wood* is his capacity to write with sympathy and joy about real
men and women.

[1] 'Lament.'
[2] W. B. YEATS: 'The Circus Animals Desertion'.

Four elements and five
Senses, and man a spirit in love,
Tangling through this spun slime
To his nimbus bell cool kingdom come. . . .

It is true, however, that because of his inability to achieve some kind of integration within himself, the resolution of conflict is often projected into some apocalyptic denouement, as in the conclusion to 'The Winters Tale':

For the bird lay bedded
In a choir of wings, as though she slept or died,
And the wings glided wide and he was hymned and wedded,
And through the thighs of the engulfing bride,
The woman breasted and the heaven headed

Bird, he was brought low,
Burning in the bride bed of love, in the whirl-
Pool at the wanting centre, in the folds
Of paradise, in the spun bud of the world.
And she rose with him flowering in her melted snow.

This is a mystical experience beyond time and what is usually considered individuality. But Thomas's later poetry does celebrate man as he is, perishing in time, but somehow imperishable. It is not an accident that someone so deeply rooted in death could write so magnificently of resurrection:

Teach me the love that is evergreen after the fall leaved
Grave, after Belovéd on the grass gulfed cross is scrubbed
Off by the sun and Daughters no longer grieved
Save by their long desires in the fox cubbed
Streets or hungering in the crumbled wood: to these
Hale dead and deathless do the women of the hill
Love for ever meridian through the courters' trees

And the daughters of darkness flame like Fawkes fires still.[1]

[1] 'In the White Giant's Thigh.'

George Barker—Vernon Watkins— W. S. Graham—David Gascoyne

O NE RESULT of the inflation, or should it be called deflation, of Literary Criticism into a science is the search for influences. It is valid enough to show how the work of one poet grows out of another, and the inter-relation of all writers in the stream of English Literature. But there is a tendency to imagine that if you have shown the relationship of a contemporary poet to an earlier one you have convicted him of plagiarism and dragged out the heart of his mystery.

It is necessary for a poet to wrestle for his own individual voice; this is part of his devotion to his craft. But individuality is a much more subtle affair than writing a poem in the shape of an hour glass or with only one word for each fifth line. Elizabethan poets could be unmistakably themselves while keeping to a very strict sonnet form. It all depends on the poet's capacity to project some essence of himself into his language. If he can do this, then since he is alive in our day, or thereabouts, his work will be contemporary even if he uses a form which was broken in ages ago, by Dante or Chaucer.

What matters is the validity of the poet's vocation, his willingness to offer the whole of himself to his verse. It is the self-conscious attempt to be original which really does become stale and dated. Setting aside poems in the shape of mice, and poems with no punctuation or metre, one suspects that many of today's most startling word-combinations and dislocations of syntax will drift into a platitudinous old age, become the purling brooks and dimpling streams of tomorrow. As for so-called 'Free Verse', it has only two great masters, Walt Whitman and D. H. Lawrence, and they were men of enormous energy. Just as water diffuses itself if it flows over a wide area like a field, but gains power and direction in a rocky bed, so poems take force from a reasonably strict metric form. Without this form they grow vapid and flabby—unless they have a sort of human dynamo like Walt Whitman behind to push them along by sheer force of personality.

George Barker (b. 1913) does infuse himself into his language, and is a truly individual poet. His work can be extremely irritating, clotted, wrong-headed, and in downright bad taste, but it is never just a clever exercise, or a kind of floral blancmange to be spooned up by the hypersensitive.

A great deal of his poetry is concerned with Eros and the guilts and ecstasies of sexual love. Sex can enable us to transcend our human limitations. Donne's poem 'The Ecstasy' is about this overpassing of individuality by the erotic experience, and many poems of Yeats and Blake are concerned with it. But the trouble is, the ecstatic experience which sexuality sets off cannot be satisfied by the act of copulation. The woman who became the symbol for so much human and more than human significance has a tendency, after sexual consummation, to become as humdrum as oneself in the role of great lover, or as yesterday's breakfast. Much of Barker's best poetry expresses this polarity between the ecstasy of sex and its dead-beat hangover.

Here is the exaltation from his first 'Sacred Elegy':

> Lovers for whom the world is always absent
> Move in their lonely union like twin stars
> Twining bright destinies around their cause:
> They dazzle to shadow with a meridian present
> The wallflower world. Redundant it shall resent
> The kiss that annihilates and the gaze that razes.
> O from their clasp a new astronomy rises
> Where, morning and evening, the dominant Venus
> Dismisses all sad worlds that turn between us,
> And we shall kiss behind our masks of faces.

And here is the morning-after hangover from *The True Confession of George Barker*:

The act of human procreation
—The rutting tongue, the grunt and shudder,
The sweat, the reek of defecation,
The cradle hanging by the bladder,
The scramble up the hairy ladder,
And from the thumping bed of Time
Immortality, a white slime,
Sucking at its mother's udder—

The serene music of the first passage is as undeniable as the force and almost pathological disgust of the second. Some such duality between bliss and revulsion is at least a stage in the human being's sense of Eros. Unless one thinks a poet should be writing for a public of eunuchs this very ubiquitous theme of Barker is of importance.

Our life is partly a question of weaning. The embryo gives up the womb to become a baby, the baby gives up its mother's breast to become a child, the child gives up its dependence on parents to become an adult. Finally the adult gives up its humanity to become goodness knows what. The point I am making is that we cannot rest at any stage of our development because life is movement and growth. Erotic desire may be an end in itself to adolescents of all ages, but ultimately it has to change and become more wide and deep, more knowledgeable, and less pin-pointed by overt sexuality and obsessions of personality. If this change does not take place then growth onwards is frustrated and Eros becomes guilt-ridden and edged with desperation. One feels just this quality of desperation about much of Barker's poetry:

Or species Ezekiel on a golden wheel
Spinning around geography to find water:
Solace of jesus-oasis, sex, or peace,
I go careering across space after them all.
O tracer bullet's scream and comet's laughter
Warn me it's useless but how can I cease.[1]

[1] 'Pacific Sonnets': No. XV.

There is hysteria and breathlessness about such writing. Like the bullet or comet the poet is a creature of an impulse he cannot control. But this impulse is not the *'La sua voluntate è nostra pace'* of Dante, the divine will which it is peace to conform to, but the compulsion of blind instinct. Barker is extremely open to this compulsion. It both fascinates and revolts him and he instils these warring emotions into his poetry:

> Aetna also. O in the sky giving the fiery lie
> To the brighter the shorter laburnum. Ah aeturnum
> Aetna agonistes. My candle is cressets, my torch is
> Bonfires in the breast, my sweat's laburnum:
> But no the cat on the hot bricks of its tortures
> Teaches me how to suffer, not how to die.[1]

I remember how, after a poetry reading, an earnest young woman said to him, 'Mr. Barker, it seems to me you have a deep sense of guilt.' 'Yes, madam,' he replied, 'it is one of my most precious possessions.' There is an honesty about this guilt, he accepts it as one aspect of the unease which is necessary for creative activity. 'You,' he once said at some earnest gathering, 'stew in your own juice, but the poet boils in his own poison'. Guilt colours much of his verse, and depends upon a realisation of the failure of his own will to correspond to a larger will of which he has a quite clear perception. Very often, though, his concern with this larger will is expressed by a frenzied and slightly delinquent revulsion against it.

> Incubus. Anaesthetist with glory in a bag,
> Foreman with a sweatbox and a whip. Asphixiator
> Of the ecstatic. Sergeant with a grudge
> Against the lost lovers in the park of creation,
> Fiend behind the fiend behind the fiend behind the
> Friend. Mastodon with mastery, monster with an ache
> At the tooth of the ego, the dead drunk judge;
> Wheresoever Thou art our agony will find Thee
> Enthroned on the darkest altar of our heartbreak
> Perfect. Beast, brute, bastard. O dog, my God![2]

[1] 'Pacific Sonnets': No. XVI.
[2] 'Sacred Elegies': No. V.

To have expressed with such ferocity this conflict within the human being is an achievement. But if a war drags on endlessly it becomes dull. It might have been a question of which came first, our boredom with George Barker's erotic excursions and morning-after guilts, or his complete exhaustion of this vein; then silence. But with the 'True Confessions' he seems to have broken out of this groove he was in, or at least out of the romanticising of his sexuality and guilts. To some extent, in this long poem, he adopts a rather cloak-and-dagger pose and cocks a childish snook at bogus authority. But, taking the poem as a whole, it is an honest self-revelation. Barker does try to strip off the deceptive nonsense with which we rationalise our less pleasant behaviour, and face up to the shadow side of himself:

> What sickening snot-engendered bastard
> Likes making an idiot of himself?
> I wish to heaven I had mastered
> The art of living like a dastard
> While still admiring oneself.
> About my doings, past and recent,
> I hear Disgust—my better half—
> 'His only decency's indecent.'[1]

This may not be the whole story, but it is an important conclusion all the same. The *True Confession* does go some way down into the 'rag and bone shop of the heart', and this descent is a condition of both poetic and personal growth. In his long and perhaps most important poem 'Goodman Jacksin and the Angel', Barker may have moved out of the circle of eroticism and guilt which was becoming repetitive. The personal conflict which his earlier verse expressed was always of general significance, but now his knowledge of it has deepened, and in this poem he may be writing from the level of experience which gives rise to the greatest poetry.

> I wake on mornings in the winter
> With the holy snow on the ground

[1] *True Confession:* Book III.

I see the hoof marks milling round
Where nightlong in the cattle pound
I and the cloven fiend, hell bound,
Wrestle together, without a sound,
For the white world that sleeps around
As we rage at the centre.[1]

In nearly every poem of George Barker we sense the man's bitter inward conflict. But Vernon Watkins (b. 1907) seems to have made some resolution of the warring opposites of flesh and spirit, time and eternity. He is a Christian poet and, like the later Eliot, concerned with the surrender of the personal will to the intention of God:

Taliesin answered: 'I have encountered the irreducible diamond
In the rock. Yet now it is over. Omniscience is not for man.
Christian me, therefore, that my acts in the dark may be just,
And adapt my partial vision to the limitation of time.[2]

The poems of Hopkins alone show how such a surrender need not make a man's work impersonal. But Vernon Watkins may wish to keep himself out of his poetry. His themes are often deeply apprehended both by emotion and intellect, and one is sure he has suffered for many of them and is only rarely versifying a sympathetic idea. Nevertheless, whether he is writing about God, or the sea, or Taliesin, the subject of the poem is usually everything. Watkins very rarely communicates to us any sense of the personal struggle which has led him as a man to choose a particular theme.

No matter how general, even transcendental, the truth which he expresses, a poet is a man speaking to other human beings, and if he irons out his humanity, then communication will be blunted. Browning, for instance, at the end of 'A Toccata of Galuppi's' brings back a long and impersonal statement about the spiritual death of Venice to the reality of himself,

[1] 'Goodman Jacksin and the Angel': *Collected Poems* (Faber).
[2] 'Taliesin and the Spring of Vision.'

'Dust and ashes!' So you creak it, and I want the heart to scold.
Dear dead women, with such hair, too—what's become of all the
    gold
Used to hang and brush their bosoms? I feel chilly and grown old.

It is just the personal, even banal, remark 'I feel chilly and grown
old' which, by fetching Browning himself into the picture, gives
to the poem the immediacy of conversation. There is a sense in
which ideas wilt without the human being who utters them;
and one of the things which distinguishes poetry from other kinds
of writing is its capacity to communicate both the speaker and
the statement which he is making.

    It is in the religious, most specifically Christian poetry of
Vernon Watkins that one feels this lack of intimacy. 'The Death
Bell' has most certainly an austere grandeur, but although it is
not overtly didactic, it has at times something of the detached
remoteness of a sermon:

> In death the fourfold man
> Still rules time's bell and can
> Teach the competitive
> The loss by which we live.
> Deep conflict is the forge
>   From which their faiths emerge
> Who give to humankind
> Mind that is more than mind

The statement of 'The Death Bell' is valid enough and so is its
cold deliberate music; what I am not certain about is Watkins's
ability to take us with him into this poem.

    However, when he writes about the coast of his native Gower,
Watkins is passionately involved with his poems and so they
are deeply moving. A bird, a piece of weathered timber, any
detail of the sea-margin which he has known for most of his life,
gives the grit of fact to his imagination and enables him fully to
embody his lofty conceptions, and bring them home to our
senses as well as the brain:

> Hidden flat on my face
> In grass, I have heard the wail
> Of bird by eel-dark bird
> Surveying the pitch and knock
> Of the breakers' punishing flail,
> Where the lightest trespassing word
> Would prompt an exodus race,
> A movement start like a shot
> Each anchorite from its mark
> To safety out in the bay.
> I have lost the light of day
> If once I have lost that dark.[1]

Given the loved and observed fact to work on, a storm or the debris of a ship-wreck, then perhaps more vividly than any living poet, Vernon Watkins can communicate the sense of a presence behind the phenomena of nature, something caught by hints and partial glimpses but never completely realised:

> Scrabbled bark, and a bone picked clean;
> Two sharp rocks, and a log between.
> Under the surface, hands unseen.
>
> Fingers picking the holes of the coast,
> Riddling water, their needle is lost;
> They quiver about us, ah haunting host![2]

Like Dylan Thomas, W. S. Graham (b. 1917) identifies himself with those forces which we sense at times behind both nature and man, and in his earlier poetry, like the earlier Dylan Thomas, he seems to have no circumference, and to merge with whatever he writes about:

> Still I pass fathom-voyaged in a volted thread
> Rigged with a stay of justice devised in fables
> Differently leaning an avalanche of kin.
> Here at this leapfrog place learning laws

---

[1] 'The Dead Shag': *The Death Bell* (Faber).
[2] 'Ballad of Hunt's Bay': *The Death Bell*.

Building an infant's alchemy of wests,
My craft with leopards at the lonely bow
Swings a long shadowed jib of proud alarms
And wakens villages and larks in scalloped cells.[1]

Man is an outward movement, and in 'The Nightfishing'
Graham tries to express the actual outgoing of ourselves from one
moment into another:

I, in Time's grace,
The grace of change, am
Cast into memory.
What a restless grace
   To trace stillness on.

To catch the mingling of present and future he identifies himself
with a ship moving out of harbour. Just as every new happening
recovers what we have always known, though lost, so the ship
walks water again, and the water is both the past and our future:

Now this place about me
Wakes the night's twin shafts
   And sheds the quay slowly.
Very gently the keel
Walks its waters again.
The sea awakes its fires.
White water stares in
From the harbour-mouth.[2]

Since we are partially determined by our past, the ship is manned
by both the dead and the living:

My dead in the crew
Have mixed all qualities
That I have been. . . .

[1] 'The Third Journey: *The Seven Journeys* (Maclellan).
[2] 'The Nightfishing': VII.

'The Nightfishing' tries to express that process of change which is perhaps the essence of human life, indeed of all life. It may well be too early to assess W. S. Graham's work, but I suspect it may be of great importance:

> This present place is
> Become made into
> A breathless still place
> Unrolled on a scroll
> And turned to face this light.

Longevity and a complete devotion to his craft, in the sense that the poet does no other job but write verses, are not always a very happy marriage. It was Wordsworth who set this fashion of exclusive devotion to the Muse, and he was followed by the two greatest Victorian poets, Tennyson and Browning. Inspiration or no, these great masters knocked out their stint of verses, and the result was, at times, many very arid pages. The trouble is that although poetry may be the chief concern of a man's life, inspiration is like the spirit, a wind-blown casual visitor, which has its own times and seasons and cannot be summoned by an act of will. Perhaps it is not always detrimental if the poet has some other job, which gives him an income, relates him to his fellow men and stops him becoming muscle-bound by a too rigorous concentration on his art. Certainly two great poets of our time, Yeats and Eliot, have been men of affairs, the one an Irish Senator and founder of a National Theatre, the other the director of a publishing house. The same is true of MacNeice and Day Lewis and—in that he also writes novels and works of imaginative scholarship—of Robert Graves. No doubt the ability to write worthwhile novels and a considerable body of good poetry is very rare indeed; for one of these forms must take over the main stream of the writer's imagination and finally squeeze the other out of existence. But a job like publishing, teaching or banking, does not use the same muscles as verse, and can help the poet to sustain the tension between the worlds of everyday reality and imagination, which is a condition of his art.

Watkins is a bank clerk; but unlike Yeats and Eliot, the other poets I have just been writing about, Thomas, Barker and W. S. Graham are committed to no other trade but their verse. Perhaps in *Under Milk Wood* Dylan Thomas had found another medium of expression which would have carried him along when his lyrical inspiration was in abeyance, and related him to the theatre. We shall never know. But although Mrs. Tennyson might ask a friend to suggest 'some pretty tender little thing which dear Alfred can turn into a copy of verses', it is unlikely that poets like George Barker or W. S. Graham would fill in the periods when imagination has deserted them by a job of versifying. Such an exclusive devotion to poetry has its dangers. Poetry feeds not only on the ecstatic moment but also on the bread of everyday event, and that is what a job forces the poet to eat, however unwillingly. Blunt fact grows dull and sour without imagination, but imagination turns into vapour unless it is continually confronted with outer fact.

One senses this split between the world of imagination and the common day in the work of David Gascoyne (b. 1916), another poet who has not been able to reconcile a trade with his poetic vocation. Perhaps such an adjustment is particularly difficult for a poet like Gascoyne, who at an early age experienced a mature but terrible insight into one aspect of life—the infernal:

> One evening like the years that shut us in,
> Roofed by dark-blooded and convulsive cloud,
> Led onward by the scarlet and black flag
> Of anger and despondency, my self:
> My searcher and destroyer: wandering
> Through unnamed streets of a great nameless town,
> As in a syncope, sudden absolute,
> Was shown the Void that undermines the world:
> For all that eye can claim is impotent—
> Sky, solid brick of buildings, masks of flesh—
> Against the splintering of that screen which shields
> Man's puny consciousness from hell: over the edge
> Of a thin inch's fraction lie in wait for him
> Bottomless depths of roaring emptiness.[1]

[1] 'Inferno.'

One is reminded of the perception of hell which Aldous Huxley tells us is sometimes induced by the taking of mescalin. And many of Gascoyne's earlier poems make such ultimate statements. It is as if the customary attitudes and conventions had been suddenly wiped off the surface of life by a corrosive acid, to expose some transcendental meaning which it is difficult for our common humanity to bear:

> 'As the shaft below began to slant
> Towards its headlong fall into unknown
> Futurity, the sacred Mouth enshrined
> Like a sarcophagus, within its midst revealed
> During that moment's timeless flash
> The wordless Meaning of the Whole
> (Which may be spoken by no man)
> Through the unearthly brilliance of its smile. . . .

> While the old world's last bonfire's turned to ash.[1]

One feels that Gascoyne has slid away from the ordinary business of living in order to obtain the insight of these poems. He makes his vision so real that it cannot be explained away; but it is the kind of revelation which might suddenly waft into us while recovering from an anaesthetic, or when in the grip of a drug.

In a later collection called *A Vagrant* Gascoyne has written verse which shows wit, tenderness and insight, and is much more relaxed than his earlier work. But I suspect it is the earlier work with its lurid glare and sense of apocalyptic revelation which is up till now his main contribution to Poetry.

[1] 'Epode'

11

A Poetry of Doubt

Most of the poets I have so far discussed have had a vision which one might call religious. I do not mean that all of them accept some particular creed; but if not directly stated it is at least implicit in their work that the human being is not wholly determined by the laws of biology or physics. In one way or another their work suggests that we are not just a dying animal working through a few revolutions of the clock before the black-out of death, because in some deep level of ourselves we are associated with a process which includes birth and death, but is not summed up by such polarities.

Perhaps it is rash to say that all great poets have shared in this open vision. In Webster and Cyril Tourneur, for example, there seems to be at first sight a kind of nihilism. From these dramatists we get the sense of all possible comforts and material refuges being ruthlessly torn away until man is brought face to face with a complete blankness. Because of its very nature they say nothing about this blankness which is the denouement of their plays. But it has always left me with the feeling of being a threshold. Thus, Webster, by divesting the Duchess of Malfi of every claim of her common humanity seems almost to waft her over this threshold into something which is neither common nor human, but, for all that, acclaimed by some fringe of our awareness, as indubitably real.

It is perfectly justifiable for Yeats to consider man as 'sick with desire and fastened to a dying animal'. The conflict between the part of oneself one knows to be material, and another reality which intuition attests to be spiritual, is a constant preoccupation of poetry. But I am doubtful whether great poetry can arise from the conception of man as nothing more than a 'dying animal'. I do not suggest for one moment that a good poet must be a doctrinaire Spiritualist, for example, or a Christian: God forbid. But I do believe that, for his work to have the necessary scope, he must realise that the human being, birth and death, are a mystery. If he tries to bring this mystery down to some purely physical explanation and make some such dogmatic statement as, 'I know what it is, a question of molecules and cells, and sad as it is, the whole bag of tricks fizzles out after a few years like a firework', then he is failing to do justice to his theme. There is simply not enough evidence for this brand of assurance. It is all very well as an incident in some larger conception, and no one can object to Macbeth's despairing rejection of life: 'It is a tale told by an idiot full of sound and fury signifying nothing.' But if such an attitude becomes the theme of a man's work, its atmosphere and conviction, then he will become unjustifiably dogmatic and consequently a minor writer. From the opposite standpoint, the same may be true of an overtly religious poet, the Trappist, Thomas Merton, for example. He knows, and a little too definitely. Without a sense of the relativity of knowledge, the mystery which all human conceptions trail off into, the poet must belittle his themes.

At times this dogmatism mars the work of a good poet, Roy Fuller (b. 1912). Although they are alive and contemporary, there is something in the attitude of his poems which reminds me of Tennyson. There is the same acute personal unease, the same anxiety of the individual threatened by the encroachment of time, and his own mortality:

> Doomed certainly, he thinks, and feels the spears
> Upon his flesh as he upturns his eyes
> Towards the yellow face of time against
> The racing sky. So this is the thing it is,
> He says aloud, to live in mortal cities—
> Haunted by trivial music, stomach tensed.[1]

Fuller does not write *about* his anxiety, but manages to bring it directly into his language. His is a limited vision perhaps; the greatest poets do, at least in their work, break through that time-fixated egotism which is the seat of anxiety. But—and again this

[1] Meredithian Sonnets: Uncollected.

is a characteristic of the Tennyson of *In Memoriam*—because Fuller is caught within himself and his dreads, there are few living poets who are so present in their work, who carry over to the reader such a sense of their own personality, and the temporal environment which encloses it:

> Great suns, the streetlamps in the pinhead rain;
> Surfaces gradually begin to shine;
> Brunettes are silvered: taxis pass in line
> On tyres that beat through moisture like a pain.
> Doubtless upon such evenings some at least
> Of those events that shaped his soul occurred:
> Against the streaming glass a whispered word
> Whitened and faded, and the shapeless beast
> Drank from the dripping gutters all the night.
> But all the child expressed and feared is long
> Forgotten: only what went wholly wrong
> Survives as this spectator of the flight
> Of lovers through the square of weeping busts
> To happiness, and of the lighted towers
> Where mad designs are woven by the powers;
> Of normal weather, ordinary lusts.[1]

This is a strong and moving expression of personal unease. Roy Fuller is aware how forces and conflicts of the past lie behind his present nervous predicament, and he admits he has not relived them and brought them into the light of day. Very few of us do, and so his stoical endurance of fear and insoluble tensions makes significant verse. It is also what gives to *In Memoriam* some of its pathos.

Earlier on I said Fuller's work was at times marred by dogmatism. When Tennyson found too much the strain between doubt and faith which we sense in some of his best poetry, he would take refuge in some religious utterance, perfectly sound in itself, but which nevertheless comes through his work as a platitude because he has probably not implemented it by personal experience:

[1] 'Meredithian Sonnets.'

That God, which ever lives and loves,
One God, one law, one element,
And one far-off divine event,
To which the whole creation moves.

I sometimes feel the final verse of *In Memoriam* is more a cheer
the poet gives to keep his courage up than a conviction he has
brought about within himself. Roy Fuller, when he is sick of the
uncertainty which characterises his work, tends to take refuge,
not in a rather inflated religious conviction, but in a materialism
which is out of keeping with his highly intelligent poetry. For
example, some of his poems suggest that Time is not one condition of our being, but an absolute. We have a small strip of it to
live in and then Finis. Thus in 'To Posterity?' he broods on the
possibility of his verse outlasting a few generations, but then gives
himself a cold douche; after all, what is the whole history of
mankind, a mere fraction of the planet's existence?—

I would wish to cheat the racing clocks,
Dials that mark the vital seventy years,
The culture's thousand, the coming lustrum's fears.

Though in such moments there of course will be
A sense of time undreamt of even by these:
Ages piled on the planet's flank that freeze
With inconceivable immobility;
And far back in the wastes the tiny span
Of the erect and big brained Primate, man.[1]

No doubt it is salutary to reflect on one's physical littleness in
comparison with the universe, or the shortness of even a millen-
nium beside the total time span of our planet, but the whole
business of size and length of time becomes irrelevant in the light
(or darkness) of Wordsworth's statement:

[1] 'To Posterity?'

> Not Chaos, not
> The darkest pit of lowest Erebus,
> Nor ought of blinder vacancy, scooped out
> By help of dreams can breed such fear and awe
> As fall upon us often when we look
> Into our minds, into the Mind of Man. . . .[1]

One cannot fob off the mystery which is a human being by talking about 'big brained Primates' (capital P) and underplaying man with a small 'm'. But at times this is the way Fuller tries to avoid his uncertainty. No doubt it is the contemporary form of Tennyson's religious panacea for *angst*. Both methods give one 'sound' information about where, and what, one is; but at the price of knowledge.

The same is true of Fuller's treatment of Myth. In the 'Mythological Sonnets' he tends to fix these ancient stories to a Freudian explanation,

> That the dread happening of myth reveal
> Our mind's disorders is a commonplace. . . .

It is important that Fuller has brought into poetry Freud's theory as to the significance of myths; this theory is vastly more relevant than the whimsical cloud-cuckoo-land where a facile rationalism had sent them packing:

> But could mere images make even now
> Ears drum with lust, the chest run secret shame?
> The myths are here: it was our father's name
> The maiden shrieked in horror as she turned
> To wrinkled bark; our dearest flesh that burned
> Straddling her legs inside a wooden cow.[2]

But myths do not only tell of sexual or aggressive desires which we have repressed because they are incompatible with our more polite daily selves. Jung has made it clear enough that they may

[1] *The Prelude.*
[2] 'Mythological Sonnets': XVII.

also express the wanderings and dangers of the human soul on its long journey. It is this traditional view of the human being which is lacking in Fuller's poetry. At times his work gives us a sense of enclosure, as if it was end-stopped by ideas which have a purely local and transient importance. However, he has expressed, and with great insight, the isolation of urban man, the feeling which we all have at times of being walled up within ourselves and the streets we live in; a mortality which is doomed, but must be endured with stoicism.

William Empson (b. 1906) is another poet who writes outside the Visionary Tradition and sees no particular meaning or intention to man's life. But there is nothing smug or comfortable in his doubt, nor does he find its vacuum intolerable and fill it up with some contemporary platitude. On the contrary, some of his best poems depend upon a passionate affirmation of uncertainty.

> All those large dreams by which men long live well
> Are magic-lanterned on the smoke of hell;
> This then is real, I have implied,
> A painted, small, transparent slide.[1]

All systems of belief are the projections of certain personal fantasies upon the smoke of hell, a chaos about which we in fact know nothing. Some fantasy or other may help us to live comfortably, but really we have no grounds for any sureness. It is possible, though, to achieve some dignity and style by accepting this vacuum:

> Feign then what's by a decent tact believed
> And act that state is only so conceived,
> And build an edifice of form
> For house where phantoms may keep warm.
>
> Imagine, then, by miracle with me,
> (Ambiguous gifts, as what gods give must be)
> What could not possibly be there,
> And learn a style from a despair.

[1] 'The Last Pain.'

It is the rather desperate honesty of statements like this, the attempt to strip the mind bare of conventional beliefs (it can degenerate into a rather 'canny' determination not to be fooled) which has made Empson a considerable influence on a number of younger poets. What also attracted them to his work was its complexity of reference and loaded ambiguity of syntax. His poems, like his books of criticism, have become a kind of treasure trove for students of English Literature to rummage about in. But the unravelling of much of his verse may depend on an interest in crossword puzzles rather than poetry:

> Spears pierce its desert basin, the long dawn:
> Tower, noon, all cliquant, dock-side cranes, sag-fruited:
> And, sand-born weight, brief by waste sand upborne,
> Leave, gulfed, ere night, the bare plain, deeper rooted.

In such a passage it is as if Empson's subtle and powerful mind had failed to connect with anything beyond itself and was grinding out a kind of metal dust. At times, though, his very inability to communicate with himself or other people produces a note of anguish which is reminiscent of Gerard Manley Hopkins:

> Slowly the poison the poison the whole blood stream fills
> It is not the effort or the failure tires.
> The waste remains, the waste remains and kills. . . .

> It is the poems you have lost, the ills
> From missing dates, at which the heart expires.
> Slowly the poison the whole blood stream fills
> The waste remains, the waste remains and kills.[1]

Hopkins's despair came from the times when he failed to communicate with his God, Empson's from his failure to touch into the wider reaches of himself and other people. One of his most direct and best known poems is about a tree whose cones can only be fertilised by a forest fire. It is an image which sums up the tragic endurance which is characteristic of his poetry.

[1] 'Missing Dates.'

Philip Larkin (b. 1922) is also unwilling to fill the vacuum of
his very fastidious doubt with any ready-made solution. But his
doubt is not so much about the outgoing into belief, as about
experience itself. That is the illusion, and he is not going to be
fooled, though to his complex sensibility even the wish not to be
fooled may be spurious:

> The trumpet's voice, loud and authoritative,
> Draws me a moment to the lighted glass
> To watch the dancers—all under twenty-five—
> Shifting intently, face to face,
> Solemnly on the beat of happiness.
>
> —Or so I fancy, sensing the smoke and sweat,
> The wonderful feel of girls. Why be out here?
> But then why be in there? Sex, yes, but what
> Is sex? Surely to think the lions' share
> Of happiness is found by couples—sheer
>
> Inaccuracy, as far as I'm concerned.

The trouble about this passage is the sly euphemism for sex: it
is simply a question of thinking the 'lion's share of happiness is
found in couples'. Of course Larkin is making a joke, and the wry
smile at himself and the 'seriousness' of human pretensions is one
of the secrets of his popularity. We are always glad to shrug
off with a laugh our stickier predicaments. But there is something
'old-maidish' in Larkin's attitude to sex, and it is part of a determination not to be caught up in any passionate human involvement, which colours all his poetry. In the poem 'Skin' he
apologises to his body because he has not allowed it the
kind of 'fling' bodies are apparently entitled to:

> And pardon me, that I
> Could find, when you were new,
> No brash festivity
> To wear you at, such as
> Clothes are entitled to
>
> Till the fashion changes. . . .

Again sex is written off; this time it is a brash festivity. But although the force of his poetry is lessened by his obvious unwillingness to come down into what Yeats called 'the frog-spawn of a blind man's ditch', Larkin can observe very acutely the suffering of others and comment on it from the standpoint of a wise and compassionate spectator. In 'Deceptions' he writes about a young girl described in Mayhew's *London Labour and the London Poor*, who was drugged and then raped.

> Slums, years, have buried you. I would not dare
> Console you if I could. What can be said,
> Except that suffering is exact, but where
> Desire takes charge, readings will grow erratic?
> For you would hardly care
> That you were less deceived, out on that bed,
> Than he was, stumbling up the breathless stair
> To burst into fulfilment's desolate attic.

Just as Beckett's play *Waiting for Godot* may appeal to lapsed Catholics who want both to have their God and reject him, so Larkin's poem 'Churchgoing' exactly catches the mood of those people who feel that our traditional religion and its churches have nearly atrophied, although, somewhere, there is a great deal more in religion and a church than the truisms they are often reduced to. He debunks the stock responses to a church, fantasies about what will be left when time has scrubbed them away, and finally tries to assess what, after all, is the meaning of such a building:

> A serious house on serious earth it is,
> In whose blent air all our compulsions meet,
> Are recognised and robed as destinies.
> And that much never can be obsolete,
> Since someone will forever be surprising
> A hunger in himself to be more serious,
> And gravitating with it to this ground,
> Which, he once heard, was proper to grow wise in,
> If only that so many dead lie round.

The deliberate understatement here depends on Larkin's determination not to sentimentalise his subject; we can have no doubt that he takes it seriously. Indeed, despite his acute scepticism, Larkin has some characteristics of a religious poet. It is true that he makes no affirmation of God, but his negation, his wish to avoid personal involvement, suggests a desire for an involvement which is impersonal or, rather, which is beyond our usual conception of personality. In the poem 'No Road' he seems to welcome the end of an attachment because of the freedom it allows him. This liberty is happening to him, although to will it to happen deliberately would be neurotic:

> A little longer
> And time will be stronger,

> Drafting a road where no such road will run
> From you to me;
> To watch that world come up like a cold sun,
> Rewarding others is my liberty.
> Not to prevent it is my will's fulfilment.
> Willing it my ailment.

Quite a number of Larkin's poems depend on a wry glance at human pretentiousness or, as in 'Maiden Name', or 'Lines on a Young Lady's Photograph Album', a rather haunting nostalgia. But there is something else looming up behind his desire not to be deceived by the ephemera of existence:

> Beyond all this, the wish to be alone.

> Beneath it all, desire of oblivion runs:
> Despite the artful tensions of the calendar,
> The life insurance, the tabled fertility rites,
> The costly aversion of the eyes from death—
> Beneath it all, desire of oblivion runs.

'Wants' is a poem of negation, but there is a raw edge of suffering to it, which we do not always find in Larkin's work. One could

say it deals with what Freud called 'the Death Wish', but that is
only a label for a direction of ourselves about which we know very
little indeed. It is probably a major theme and one capable of
much understanding. This quotation from a poem called 'Next
Please' may show how effectively Larkin can express this dark
purpose of human life. Ships heave up towards us from the
horizon, and we think they are cargoed with all we could possibly
want. They are quite illusory except the last vessel which really
is seeking for us:

> We think each one will heave to and unload
> All good into our lives, all we are owed
> For waiting so devoutly and so long.
> But we are wrong:
>
> Only one ship is seeking us, a black-
> Sailed unfamiliar, towing at her back
> A huge and birdless silence. In her wake
> No waters breed or break.

12

In the Fifties

IN THIS last chapter I shall be concerned mainly with poets who began to make their impact in the Fifties. With the exception of Stevie Smith and Patrick Kavanagh, older poets whom I have kept to the end because their work has not yet received the acceptance which it deserves, it is too early to pontificate about these writers. In most cases there is not enough of it above ground to give an idea of its eventual shape and stature. This lack of an achieved body of work has its critical dangers. Shoots which on their first appearance were of an exciting green and occasioned raptures in the Sunday papers and on the B.B.C., may after a few more years turn into a particularly dreary and domestic vegetable.

Often the first appeal of a new writer of verse depends on his having picked up some of the gestures and verbal felicities of a fairly recent and widely accepted poet. This similarity may be the right and inevitable development of one poet from another. On the other hand it can be parasitism. Until a poet has written a good deal of work, it is difficult to know whether he has some distinctive vision which he is struggling to fulfil with all the resources of the language, or is merely turning verses, with no deeper inspiration than a certain taste for words and interest in literature. Paradoxically, the work of poets who have only this bogus, literary inspiration behind them may—for a comparatively short time—give an impression of force and originality. Because they are used by no particular vision, they have very little to say, consequently their energy can be almost entirely absorbed by ways of saying. As they have nothing to say of importance they can devote themselves almost exclusively to the pattern and texture of language. It often takes considerable time for us to realise that there is either nothing at all behind the drapery, or some comfortable platitude. It is not unpleasant to meet such old acquaintances dressed up fit to kill, so this brand of verse will always 'make friends and influence people'.

As opposed to this kind of parasitic writing it may happen that where a young poet has been taken hold of by some definite vision, he will be so anxious to put across what it has to say that he will use, in a rather slapdash way, some of the mannerisms of other writers as a short cut to communication. A distinctive theme, however, demands distinctive speech if it is to come to grips with its age, and the poet will have to iron out such archaisms. Granted the exacting demands of some vision, he will forge almost inevitably an individual and appropriate diction. Style is a consequence of this imperative. One can as easily think of a beautiful dress walking the street without a body, as a fine style which serves no important theme. All such a divorce can result in is preciousness and literary anaemia.

Poetry, I have already said, is not just a question of an aptitude for words and the ability to respond with intelligence and sympathy to the various problems of the age. This may occasion some good journalistic verse with a wide appeal, but for poetry there must be an involvement with the subject in depth. To write effectively about some happening of the external world, the poet must understand it with the same kind of inward knowledge that he has of himself. In this sense a poet's exploration of an event—however remote from him in space—is always an exploration of himself. If there is not this at-oneness between subject and object, history and autobiography, then he will tend to produce a kind of verse journalism, and it will usually be didactic. This distinction is well illustrated by the work of Christopher Logue (b. 1926) and John Wain (b. 1925), two young writers who are both concerned with our contemporary problems. For all the ostensible energy of his language, Logue stands outside these problems. One does not feel that he has implimented his Marxist slogans and strictures within himself; on the contrary, he seems to have made them a substitute for personal experience. Since he has left himself out of the picture, his verse expresses only a half truth and has the hectoring tone of the popular pulpit. John Wain, on the other hand, writes about contemporary events with self knowledge and consequently with some humility and compassion. His 'A Song About Major Eatherly' tells about the pilot of the aircraft which carried the second atomic bomb to Nagasaki. Eatherly seems to have gone into a state of depression and mental instability as a result of this mission, but he refused to touch the state pension which was awarded him, and was later sent to prison for petty theft. Wain's poem does associate both himself and all of us with this one man's fate:

> O, give his pension to the storekeeper,
> Tell him it is the price of all our souls.
> But do not trouble to unlock the door
> And bring the Major out into the sun.
> Leave him: it is all one: perhaps his nightmares
> Grow cooler in the twilight of the prison.
> Leave him; if he is sleeping come away.
> But lay a folded paper by his head,
> Nothing official or embossed, a page
> Torn from your notebook, and the words in pencil.
> Say nothing of love, or thanks, or penitence:
> Say only 'Eatherly, we have your message'.

With eight other poets of the Fifties, some earlier work of John Wain was included in an anthology called *New Lines*, edited by Robert Conquest. Conquest tried to say something about the quality of this contemporary verse in his introduction. 'If one had briefly to distinguish the poetry of the fifties from its predecessors, I believe the most important general point would be that it submits to no great systems of theoretical constructs nor agglomeration of unconscious demands. It is free from both mystical and logical compulsions and—like modern philosophy— is empirical in its attitude to all that comes. This reverence for the real person or event is, indeed, a part of the general intellectual ambience of our time.'

Imagination need not falter at just how arid verse would be which 'submits to no agglomeration of unconscious demands,' for we have many examples of it. No doubt Conquest is tilting at poets like Dylan Thomas, George Barker and W. S. Graham with this remark, and it is true that their earlier work sometimes gives the impression that they believed whatever came bubbling out of the unconscious was a poetic truth which had no need of the interpreting intellect to bring it home to the reader. But in their later work these poets do realise the need for interpretations and struggle for greater lucidity. The *New Lines* writers are following a tendency which was already in existence in their attempt to produce poems which can stand up to a cold daylight scrutiny. However, as D. J. Enright says, 'Clarity may be a pleasant change after obscurity—but it can have no real meaning unless it is being clear about something.'[1] One feels this quatrain of Roy Campbell applies to the work of some makers of contemporary verse:

> You praise the firm restraint with which they write
> I'm with you there of course,
> They use the snaffle and the bit alright,
> But where's the bloody horse?

How long this stricture will apply is another matter. The growing pains a poet had to work through in the 1890s were the roses and great violet eyes and twilights of that period. Today it is a rather irritating and prudish suspicion of passionate feeling, and a determination to be worthy and unfooled. This is probably only a stage which the poets among these writers will soon outgrow. Elizabeth Jennings (b. 1926) was included in *New Lines*, and she has already shed a great deal of the primness and rather chilly detachment which characterised her earlier work. Her subjects have always been important—self-exploration, the mystery of identity, love; but at first she did not seem sufficiently taken up by them and remained the aloof observer. Here is the first verse of a poem of hers called 'Identity'. Ostensibly it is about love, but she seems to draw a diagram of the experience on a blackboard, then comment on it with a well-modulated voice, and point out interesting bits with a neat forefinger. A polished performance, but it lacks force, and so, despite its technical smoothness, there is little life in the poem:

[1] 'Criticism for Criticism's Sake': *The Apothecary's Shop* (Secker and Warburg)

When I decide I shall assemble you
Or more precisely, when I decide which thoughts
Of mine about you fit most easily together,
Then I can learn what I have loved, what lets
Light through the mind. The residue
Of what you may be goes.

.   .   .   .   .

So then assemble me,
Your exact picture firm and credible,
Though as I think myself I may be free
And accurate enough.
That you love what is truthful to your will
Is all that ever can be answered for
And, what is more,
Is all we make each other when we love.

Elizabeth Jennings has steadily closed in to the emotional life of
her poetry and sloughed off her rather cold remoteness. In
poems like 'Requiem' she combines technical skill with sincere
thought and feeling:

It is the ritual not the fact
That brings a held emotion to
Its breaking point. This man I knew
Only a little; by his death
Shows me a love I thought I lacked
And all the stirrings underneath.

It is the calm, the solemn thing,
Not the distracted mourner's cry
Or the cold place where dead things lie,
That teaches me I cannot claim
To stand aside. These tears which sting—
Are they from sorrow or from shame?

The development of any poet should warn one against the
danger of premature generalisation. Although it is easy to be wise
after the event, I suspect it would be difficult to say much about

the stature of Yeats from his first two volumes. It is with this reservation that I mention the work of Dr. Donald Davie, a writer of verse whose work seems to be parasitic, in that it derives not so much from the whole man struggling with himself and the world about him, as from the critical intellect, assessing the experience of others, nipping its own neatly in the bud, and then gumming down the result like a dead insect on a piece of clean paper.

No one would wish to deny the skill with which Dr. Davie (b. 1922) constructs his neat verse patterns with their flavour of the eighteenth century, or the sharpness of his mind. But poetry does not depend only on using words with precision and good taste. It must also have something to say, and what it says must be of some importance, whether it is about God, man, or man's environment. I do not mean that poetry should always be harping solemnly upon the eternal verities, but if it does not give us some illumination of ourselves, a widening or clarification of the turbulent process of living, then the art is reduced to a mere kill-time, about as important as a musical box or cross-word puzzle.

It would be unfair to say that Davie's work is only this. But in poem after poem I find myself following—quite eagerly, for his verse is well-made—a series of logical remarks, to be left at the end of the journey with a thin nail-paring of significant meaning. It is interesting that many of his poems are based on the work of other people. He has written verse about the writers of the Thirties, pictures by Daniel O'Neil and Juan Gris, or an engraving of Piranesi, and more recently has made an adaption of the Polish epic, *Pan Tadeusz*, a work which has already achieved two English translations. Davie seems to me to be a writer of much technical skill but no particular vision of his own, and it is significant that he has devoted his last book to the adaptation of a foreign poet into contemporary English.

D. J. Enright (b. 1920) is the antithesis of a cloistered poet. In his critical book, *The Apothecary's Shop*, he attacks the scientific abstraction and withdrawal from the human centre which he believes is characteristic of many aspects of modern life. 'Political formulas, ever hardening, are forcing out the notion of our common humanity; in the best of our contemporary poetry a querulous and donnish wit mocks redundantly at the "still sad music of humanity"; and the narrow sophistication of our literary criticism further encourages the substitution of the shadow for the reality.'

Many of his poems combat this whittling away of the human being in favour of an abstraction, a process which, of course, leaves the human being exactly as he is, but divorces poetry from its proper relevance to the life of man:

> The peasants have salvaged their cabbages; the block
> of flats is nearly as ready as its tenants; somewhere
> someone saves a child from a swollen river,
> and really means it—
> the critics in their studies, collate as ever
> their absence of meanings, unvexing and unvexed—
> but the grass waves high on the road again
> and the roots refer to the text.

Enright is an itinerant poet and his verse records, without much gloss or theory, the life he has known in Egypt or Japan or Bangkok. His writing is often angular and rough, as if he feels a too formal pattern would somehow devitalise his subject. At first sight one might suspect that his verse is of one dimension only, that it records the striking event but does not show how it touches over (as all events do) into wider areas of meaning, a good and evil of which it is a metaphor. But I think this first impression is false, for Enright manages to fetch into his near-reportage verse, hints of this further significance. 'Am Steinplatz', for example, though not a particularly good example of his work, does show how even his baldest reportage can invest a very small incident with menacing undertones. The poem is about a visit to a park in Berlin where there are memorials to the recent German dead.

> Remember those whom Hitlerism killed
> Remember those whom Stalinism killed
>
> Requests the stone by which you leave.

A dog jumps on the bench beside me.
Nice doggie: never killed a single Jew or Gentile.
Then it jumps on me. Its paws are muddy, muzzle wet.
Gently I push it off. It likes this game of war.

At last a neat stout lady on a nearby bench
Calls tenderly, 'Komm, Liebchen, komm!
Der Herr'—this public-park-frau-barks—
'does not like dogs!'

Shocked papers rustle to the ground;
Ices drip away forgotten, sleepers awake:
The lovers mobilise their distant eyes.
The air strikes cold
There's no room for a third stone here.
I leave.

There is room for all sorts of comment here, no rhyme, no
rhythm worth speaking of, the thing is not a poem at all. Such
strictures may very well be justified, but whatever class this
example of Enright's work comes into, it is alive. That is a
great relief after so much current verse which is correctly dressed
but quite moribund.

Enright rarely writes about himself directly, although his
personality emerges clearly enough from the very distinctive
attitude which he has to his subjects. Recently, however, he
has written poems which are concerned with his inner mood.
One of them is called 'Saying No' and typically it seeks to remove
the various verbal tricks with which we slur over our real needs,
and to face the vacuum, the blankness of ourselves, which we
usually try to fill up with little 'treats' and pleasantries.

After so many (in so many places) words,
It came to this one, No,
Epochs of parakeets, of peacocks, of paradisial birds—
Then one bald owl creaked, No.

And now (in this one place, one time) to celebrate
One sound will serve. . . .
Just, No.

Some virtue here, in this speech stupefied inane,
To keep it short.
However cumbrous, puffed and stretched the pain—
To say no more than, No.

John Heath Stubbs (b. 1918) has produced several volumes of verse and at first sight his work appears to have a rather faded and 'romantic' diction. 'Cold distant fires', 'Love . . . the last illusion': he often uses phrases which seem quite outmoded. But I think this is a superficial impression, for Stubbs takes care to discipline his language by some ironic twist or dry, casual word, and so bring it to heel in the present day. Usually this poet expresses himself through personae taken from myth or history, and his characters seem to need the apparent archaism of his language for their vitality, which is both historical and yet of this day and age. What matters is the life which Stubbs breathes into his personae. He appends this note to his poem 'Titus and Berenice': 'According to Jewish tradition, Titus was afflicted with an insect in his brain as punishment for his destruction of the temple'. I expect that is accurate, but like so much of Stubbs's work, this poem is interesting for the extraordinarily vivid way in which its legendary characters express sexual guilt and the sense of having betrayed some sacred purpose of life. Somehow it is the very remoteness of his protagonists, in time, which makes us realise how inescapable and always present are certain feelings, and their patterns of behaviour:

> 'In darkness master me,
> Rome with your seven hills,
> Roads, rhetorical aqueducts,
> And ravaging eagles;
> Worlds are at bitter odds, yet we
> Can find our love at least—
> Not expedient to the Senate,
> Abominable to the priest.'

155

Titus, the clement Emperor
And she of Herod's house
Slobbered and clawed each other
Like creatures of the stews;
Lay together, then lay apart
And knew they had not subdued—
She the insect in his brain
Nor he her angry god.

In Michael Hamburger (b. 1924) one senses the conflict between the critical intellect—he is a university lecturer—and whatever more intuitive, chaotic areas of a human being poetry comes from. Perhaps Donald Davie is in the same predicament, but unlike Davie, the poet in Hamburger wins the struggle. I suspect it is a bitter struggle, but although it may reduce his output of verse, it also gives to some of his poems an extraordinary fusion of emotion and thought. In 'Palinode', for example, Hamburger not only explores himself, but makes a most searching enquiry into the creative process, the way feeling is drawn off into a work of art at the price of human relationship:

Recant, recant the tenderness
That flows too easily. Confess:
Well shod against the jagged stalk
We tender-footed poets walk
On horrors multiple as grass,
A luscious carpet—pause, but pass:
And like the matador's, our skill
Is wasted if we cannot kill.
Loud in the weather-vane
Unfeeling winds complain.

Kill every creature, beast and bird,
Flower and ourselves, to feed the Word,
Our last Chimera never found
Till we have covered desert ground
With serpents, goats and lions killed
For the one site on which to build

An egocentric heap of stones
Inscribed: Bellerophon—his bones.
Yet not for so much gain:
Vanished summits we attain.

In his 'Mathematics of Love' there is the same blend of almost
clinical observation and deep feeling as he examines the relationship between man and woman, promiscuity and fidelity:

Deep in the hell where Don Juan
Knows he has added names in vain
Since all the aggregate is lost
To him not widowed but a ghost,
While those bereaved of one possess
A minus greater than his plus.

True love begins with algebra,
Those casual actors X and Y,
Nonentities whose magic role
Is to turn nothing into all,
To be and not to be, to mate:
The links are chance, the chain is fate.

There is a lasting quality about the best of Hamburger's poetry,
but I suspect its public will probably be in depth through time.

Charles Causley (b. 1917), on the other hand, may be that
rare creature, a good popular poet. He uses the traditional
rhythms of ballad and song, and his images flash with a colour and
sweetness which is at times too obvious and delightful. But
despite lapses into bathos and whimsy, Causley does not wear his
poetical properties like borrowed clothes, they really do suit
him, and, what is more, he can use them for a serious purpose.
At his best, as in 'The Great Sun', or 'The Ballad of the Five
Continents', he treats of some major themes of poetry, the
enduring life-spring which underlies our daily selves, the knowledge which pierces through the ephemera of existence:

In blue Bristol city at tall-tide I wandered
Down where the sea-masts their signals were shining,
I heard a proud seaman on the poop-deck reclining
Shout to the stars that about the ship blundered
On the high harbour lie six shifty daughters
Their bodies are straight, their eyes are wide
Here is the key of their burly bedchamber
I have unlocked it, I replied.

As I walked in Wine street the silk snow was falling
As night in her Asian hair hung her comb,
Soft sang the yellow-faced seamen of home
The gong and coconut-fiddle recalling
In the vermilion forest the dancer
Adorns with gold thorns his holy head
Will you not seize his hands, his fingers?
I am the dance, I said.[1]

More than most other contemporary poets, the work of Patrick Kavanagh and R. S. Thomas is associated with a particular landscape. I do not mean it has a regional, guide-book interest, or merely presents 'local worthies', interesting but a trifle remote from modern life. It is not a question of the poet knowing many people and many places, but of knowledge in depth. This both Thomas and Kavanagh possess, and the fact that their vision is rooted in one particular soil, gives it an exceptional firmness of contour and sense of person and place.

R. S. Thomas (b. 1913) is a clergyman of North Wales and like Wordsworth's his poetry can express the endurance, the blend of drabness and grandeur which he finds in some human beings. His hill farmers have often been withered up and spiritually starved, but they have the dignity and toughness of the boulders and thorn trees among which they work.

> Iago Prytherch, forgive my naming you.
> You are so far in your small fields
> From the world's eye, sharpening your blade
> On a cloud's edge, no one will tell you

[1] 'Ballad of Five Continents.'

How I made fun of you, or pitied either
Your long soliloquies, bent at your slow
And patient surgery under the faint
November rays of the sun's lamp.

.   .   .   .   .

Fun? Pity? No word can describe
My true feelings. I passed and saw you
Labouring there, your dark figure
Marring the simple geometry
Of the square fields with its gaunt question.
My poems were made in its long shadow
Falling coldly across the page.[1]

In 'Evans', Thomas describes his visit as a priest to a dying man
who is stranded by illness. There is an acute sense of desolation
in poems like this, but they are not simply pessimistic, concerned
with nothing more than man as a dying animal. The bed on
which Evans is stranded is likened to a shore, and this faint
association with departure, just opens the poem from its concentration on human wreckage, and so gives it a wider scope:

It was the dark filling my eyes
And mouth apalled me: not the drip
Of rain like blood from the one tree
Weather-tortured. It was the dark
Silting the veins of that sick man
I left stranded upon the vast
And lonely shore of his bleak bed.

I must not give the impression that R. S. Thomas's work is
confined to his parishioners. This short poem called 'Pisces', with
its blend of gaiety and earnestness, shows another quality of
his verse:

Who said to the trout,
You shall die on Good Friday
To be food for a man
And his pretty lady?

[1] 'Iago Prytherch'

It was I, said God,
Who formed the roses
In the delicate flesh
And the tooth that bruises.

Patrick Kavanagh was born fifty years ago in County Monaghan, and though he now lives in Dublin much of his poetry is steeped in the atmosphere of the farm where he grew up and worked:

My hills hoard the bright shillings of March
While the sun searches in every pocket.
They are my Alps and I have climbed the Matterhorn
With a sheaf of hay for three perishing calves
In a field under the big fort of Rocksavage.

The sleety winds fondle the icy beards of Shancoduff
While the cattle drovers sheltering in the Featherna Bush
Look up and say; 'Who owns them hungry hills
That the water-hen and the snipe must have forsaken?
A poet? Then by heavens he must be poor.'
I hear and is my heart not bitterly shaken.

Whether he is writing with the conversational ease of that poem 'Shancoduff', or the extreme compression of the quatrain, 'Sanctity', Kavanagh seems to carry himself right over into his poems; consequently they are always alive and very often moving:

To be a poet and not know the trade,
To be a lover and repel all women:
Twin ironies by which great saints are made,
The agonising pincer jaws of heaven.

It is an extraordinary achievement to have charged those four short lines with such an intensity of thought and feeling. The statement is perfectly clear and direct and yet could sustain an extremely lengthy paraphrase.

It is true in some of Kavanagh's work he is busily airing the chip on his shoulder, growling at people who have annoyed him and he can let us down with a shattering bathetic thump. But very often he breaks free from his private obsessions into poetry which is both innocent and extremely mature. The world is not so much transfigured—there is none of Gascoyne's mescalin glare about it, or Muir's crystalline dream—as restored by Kavanagh's verse. He seems to bring it back to a truth it has always had, but which we lose sight of because of the blinkers we wear, our timid need to curtail the scope of awareness. Some of his best poems are a kind of celebration of 'what is':

> Leafy-with-love banks and the green waters of the canal
> Pouring redemption for me, that I do
> The will of God, wallow in the habitual, the banal
> Grow with nature now as before I grew.
> The bright stick trapped, the breeze adding a third
> Party to a couple kissing on an old seat,
> And a bird gathering materials for the nest for the Word
> Eloquently new and abandoned to its delirious beat.[1]

The bird that Kavanagh writes about there is real enough; yet it is gathering material to make a nest for the Word. It is by such a slight twist of language and not by any heavy sermonising that he is able to suggest the unfathomable significance of living creatures.

Reviewers often mention the apparent artlessness of Stevie Smith's work, as if she were the perpetual child of English verse, writing poems which have a precocious child's insight into the adult world and a certain naive felicity, but which can be dismissed as fundamentally unserious. Such a view ignores the acute observation of her best poems, their technical skill, their balance between comedy and tragedy, and concentrates on the lunatic fringe of verse which undoubtedly surrounds them. This fringe is extremely broad: one could pick out of her work enough 'pussy-cats' and 'funny-faces' to make a whole volume of undiluted whimsy. But although her critical sense may be a

[1] 'Canal Bank Walk': *Come Dance with Kitty Stobling* (Longmans).

rather chancy affair, which can let some very odd creatures indeed on to the printed page, when it is working well and her imagination is at full stretch, the penetration and originality of Stevie Smith's work and its mature simplicity make such strictures quite irrelevant:

> Nobody heard him, the dead man,
> But still he lay moaning:
> I was much further out than you thought
> And not waving but drowning.
>
> Poor chap, he always loved larking
> And now he's dead
> It must have been too cold for him his heart gave way
> They said.
>
> Oh, no no no, it was too cold always
> (Still the dead one lay moaning)
> I was much too far out all my life
> And not waving but drowning.[1]

Finally two younger poets whose work has vigour and inventiveness both of conception and form which suggests great possibilities of development, though it is too early to know very much about its eventual shape and direction. Patricia Beer (b. 1917) included in her first collection a long poem about shipwreck, called 'The Loss of the Magyar'. It is an extremely haunting blend of tragic dignity and compassion, and contains passages of great insight into the process of dying:

> Each man sums up the seas
> Alone; as rings in trees
> Measure the time it takes
> To die, so white as wax
> Float all their hoops of breath.
> Drowning is a long growth
> For men to take to death.

[1] 'Not Waving but Drowning.'

Drowning is but a face,
Without age, without peace,
The answer water gives
To every man that lives
Through the last question. Sea
Yielding and bent, can be
Stiffer than wharf or quay.

There is the same sense of potential and strength about the work of Ted Hughes (b. 1930), a poet who finds an image for the passionate, intuitive energies of life in hawks and fish and otters. Beasts are a dangerous subject, and a poet who writes about them can easily produce a kind of tame zoo. But Hughes's creatures do illuminate human experience; his Otter is a very powerful symbol for the questing night-time element in ourselves which cannot be domesticated:

Does not take root like the badger. Wanders, cries;
Gallops along land he no longer belongs to;
Re-enters the water by melting.

Of neither water or land. Seeking
Some world lost when first he dived, that he cannot come at
    since,
Takes his changed body into the holes of lakes;
As if blind, cleaves the stream's push till he licks
The pebbles of the source; from sea

To sea crosses in three nights
Like a king in hiding. . . .

.   .   .   .   .

That is the end of this critique of contemporary verse, and it has left out a number of poets of obvious quality. I did not wish to re-hash the critical judgments of other people too much, consequently it was only possible to discuss verse which had come through to me with some immediacy, whether I liked it, or quite the opposite. Either way it is a personal response and poems have no other place to live in.

Since the death of Yeats and the silence, as far as poetry goes, of T. S. Eliot, critics sometimes remark how lively and intelligent is the contemporary landscape, but of course it contains no major poet. Major poet, though, is a posthumous term and much better reserved for the illustrious dead. One must remember the Elizabethan who summed up his contemporary scene with 'the right happy and copious industry of Master X, Y, Z and William Shakespeare'. What may be true is that every age has its especial brand of anti-poetry. When Wordsworth and Coleridge began to write, it was the metronomic beat of the heroic couplet, the attempt to abstract man from his essential mystery, and reduce nature to a painted backcloth. For T. S. Eliot it was sentimentalism, verse which mimicked an emotion it had not paid for in terms of experience. I suggest that what is most hostile to poetry in our present day is the attempt to narrow its scope and significance.

Poetry is not an ingenious exercise in semantics best practised by very clever people, an arrangement of beautiful noises, or a delightful game, isolated from the real life to which it bears little reference; nor is it a jolly gloss on the serious truths which have been discovered by science. It is one of the chief ways by which we are able to explore the world of our inward experience and that of other people; it also says something about the significance of natural phenomena, which cannot be understood in terms of chemistry or mathematics. As opposed to verse about verse, etchings and rubber-ducks, poetry does try to sustain and recreate a living unity of thought and feeling. It also gives a local habitation and a name to the strange and savage fauna within us. I can think of few activities which are so important, for it is becoming quite obvious that on our waking up to the fact that we have a psyche which conditions our behaviour, depends whether or not we have a future.

INDIVIDUAL AND COLLECTED
BOOKS OF VERSE

AUDEN, W. H.

Collected Shorter Poems. Faber, 1950.
Nones. Faber, 1952.
The Shield of Achilles. Faber, 1955.

BARKER, GEORGE.

Collected Poems. Faber, 1957.
The True Confession of George Barker.
Parton Press, 1957.

BEER, PATRICIA.

The Loss of the Magyar. Longmans, 1959.

BETJEMAN, JOHN.

Collected Poems. Murray, 1958.

CAUSLEY, CHARLES.

Survivors Leave. Hand and Flower Press,
1953.
Union Street. Hart–Davis, 1957.

DAVIE, DONALD

Brides of Reason. Fantasy Press, 1955.
A Winter Talent. Routledge, 1957.
The Forests of Lithuania. Marvell Press,
1959.

DAY LEWIS, C.

Collected Poems. Cape, 1957. Faber, 1936.

ELIOT, T. S.

Collected Poems 1909–1935.
Four Quartets. Faber, 1944.

EMPSON, WILLIAM.

Collected Poems. Chatto and Windus,
1955.

ENRIGHT, D. J.

The Laughing Hyena. Routledge, 1953.
Bread Rather Than Blossoms. Secker and
Warburg, 1956.
Some Men Are Brothers. Chatto, 1960

FULLER, ROY.

Epitaphs and Occasions. Lehmann, 1949.
Brutus's Orchard. Andre Deutsch, 1958.

GASCOYNE, DAVID

Poems 1937–1942. Poetry, London, 1943.
A Vagrant. Lehmann, 1950.

GRAHAM, W. S.   *The Seven Journeys*. Maclellan, 1944.
The Nightfishing. Faber, 1955.

GRAVES, ROBERT.   *Collected Poems*. Cassell, 1959.

HAMBURGER, MICHAEL.   *Poems*. Hand and Flower Press, 1951.
The Dual Site. Routledge, 1958.

HEATH STUBBS, JOHN.   *A Charm Against the Toothache*. Methuen, 1954.
The Triumph of the Muse. O.U. Press, 1958.

HUGHES, TED.   *The Hawk in the Rain*. Faber, 1957.
Lupercal. Faber, 1960.

JENNINGS, ELIZABETH.   *Poems*. Fantasy Press, 1953.
A Way of Looking. Deutsch, 1958.

KAVANAGH, PATRICK.   *A Soul for Sale*. Macmillan, 1947.
Come Dance With Kitty Stobling. Longmans, 1960.

LARKIN, PHILIP.   *The Less Deceived*. Marvell Press, 1955.

LOGUE, CHRISTOPHER.   *Songs*. Hutchinson, 1959.

MACNEICE, LOUIS.   *Collected Poems, 1925–1948*. Faber, 1949.
Autumn Sequel. Faber, 1954.
Visitations. Faber, 1957.

MUIR, EDWIN.   *Collected Poems*. Faber, 1960.

OWEN, WILFRED.   *Poems*. Chatto and Windus, 1931.

POUND, EZRA.   *The Pisan Cantos*. Faber, 1949.
Seventy Cantos. Faber, 1950.
Personae. Faber, 1952.
The Cantos. Faber, 1954.

RAINE, KATHLEEN.   *Collected Poems*. Hamish Hamilton, 1956.

SITWELL, EDITH.   *Collected Poems*. Macmillan, 1957.

SMITH, STEVIE.   *Mother What is Man*. Cape, 1942.
Harold's Leap. Chapman and Hall, 1950.
Not Waving But Drowning. Deutsch, 1957.

SPENDER, STEPHEN.	*Collected Poems.* Faber, 1955.
THOMAS, DYLAN.	*Collected Poems.* Dent, 1952.
THOMAS, R. S.	*Song at the Year's Turning.* Hart–Davis, 1955.
	Poetry for Supper. Hart–Davis, 1958.
WAIN, J.	*A Word Carved on a Sill.* Routledge, 1956.
WATKINS, VERNON.	*Ballad of the Mari Lwyd.* Faber, 1941.
	The Death Bell. Faber, 1954.
	Cyprus and Acacia. Faber, 1959.
YEATS, W. B.	*Collected Poems.* Macmillan, 1950.

Index